Regardless of the source of the client's emotional claustrophobia, this volume, a creative synthesis of cognitive, behavioral, and dynamic theories, teaches how overwhelmed, guilt-ridden people, whose fears petrify them because they expect to lose self in relationships, can achieve trust and intimacy, manage their bodies' sensations, take charge of their minds, and devise a plan to gain psychological freedom, and then live by that constructed formula. I highly recommend this book to therapists and clients alike; it is a must-read book, a therapy-driven, self-help resource, expertly balanced, clear and concise, client-usable and friendly, and therapeutically insightful.

—**Erwin Randolph Parson, Ph.D.**
Former Editor-In-Chief, *Journal of Contemporary Psychotherapy*, and psychologist with the War Stress/Trauma Recovery Program, Baltimore Veterans Affairs Medical Center, VAMHCS

Emotional Claustrophobia

Getting Over Your Fear
of Being Engulfed by
People or Situations

Aphrodite Matsakis, Ph.D.

New Harbinger Publications, Inc.

Publisher's Note

This publication is designed to provide accurate and authoritative information in regard to the subject matter covered. It is sold with the understanding that the publisher is not engaged in rendering psychological, financial, legal, or other professional services. If expert assistance or counseling is needed, the services of a competent professional should be sought.

Distributed in the U.S.A. by Publishers Group West; in Canada by Raincoast Books; in Great Britain by Airlift Book Company, Ltd.; in South Africa by Real Books, Ltd.; in Australia by Boobook; and in New Zealand by Tandem Press.

Copyright © 2000 by Aphrodite Matsakis
               New Harbinger Publications, Inc.
               5674 Shattuck Avenue
               Oakland, CA 94609

Cover design © 2000 by Lightbourne Images
Edited by Angela Watrous
Text design by Tracy Marie Powell

ISBN 1-57224-211-6 Paperback

All Rights Reserved

Printed in the United States of America

New Harbinger Publications' Web site address: www.newharbinger.com

02   01   00

10   9   8   7   6   5   4   3   2   1

First printing

Contents

Acknowledgments   ix

Introduction   1

Emotional Claustrophobia: A Common Dilemma
• Costs of Emotional Claustrophobia • Causes of
Emotional Claustrophobia • Empowerment and the
Empowerment Process • The Crisis of Recovery
• Is This Book for You? • How to Use This Book
• How This Book Is Organized • The Value of
Writing about Painful Experiences • A Final Note

Part I
Understanding Emotional Claustrophobia

Chapter 1   Did Your Family Contribute?   17

Parents and Caregivers • Physical and Sexual
Abuse • Emotional Abuse • Was Your Privacy
Invaded? • Jealousy and Possessiveness • Were
You Expected to Do or Be the Impossible? • When
Close Is Too Close • Were You Trapped in an
Emotional Tug-of-War? • Self-Assessment for
Triangulation • Family Hardships

Chapter 2   Did People or Events Outside Your   **55**
                Family Contribute?

Were You Ever Victimized or Traumatized?
• Do You Have Difficulties Setting Boundaries?
• All-or-Nothing Organizations and Belief Systems
• Difficult Human Emotions • Grief • Engulfing
Personalities

Chapter 3   How Has Emotional Claustrophobia   **71**
                Impacted Your Life?

The Importance of a Personal Inventory
• Beginning Your Inventory • Fear of Engulfment
Inventory

Chapter 4   Do Your Fears Belong to the Past   **85**
                or the Present?

Causes of Your Emotional Claustrophobia • How
Valid Are the Causes Today? • Action Steps for
Certain Causes

Chapter 5   Managing Your Anxiety   **95**

How Anxiety Can Affect Your Physical and
Mental Powers • Your Physical Reactions to Fear
• Techniques for Managing Anxiety • Medication

Chapter 6   Taking Charge of Your Mind: **109**
                Evaluating Your Beliefs

How Thoughts and Feelings Relate • Challenging
Untrue Beliefs • Identifying Your Self-Defeating
Beliefs • Which of Your Beliefs Are Self-Defeating?
• Desired Beliefs

Part II
Identifying Self-Defeating Beliefs

Chapter 7   Making a Plan   **125**

Why You Need a Plan • How to Make a Plan
• Communication Skills • Connected but Free:
Maintaining Connection without Engulfment
• Emergency Plans • Anticipating the Worst

Chapter 8 Living Your Plan   **145**

Before You Try Out Your Plan • Coping Methods
During the Event • Reviewing Your Progress

Appendix   **157**

Anger Management • Battering—Family Violence
• Child Abuse • Guidelines for Interacting with/
Confronting Abusive Family Members • Depression
• Rape and Sexual Assault • Relaxation: Anxiety
and Panic Disorders Management • Self-Esteem
and Assertiveness • Trauma Processing

References   **163**

Acknowledgments

I would like to acknowledge both Angela Watrous for her excellent editorial revisions and the staff at New Harbinger Publications for their support during the writing of this book. I would also like to thank Peter Valerio, M.A., C.P.C., for his insights into the struggles of persons suffering from emotional claustrophobia. Most of all, however, I would like to thank those clients who have trusted me enough to share their struggles with emotional claustrophobia with me. These individuals have struggled to contribute to their families, friends, and communities and make a positive difference in the lives of others, despite the anxiety and paralysis caused by their fear of engulfment. They are all on the path to managing their fear of engulfment so that they can engage in activities and relationships more freely than they ever dreamed possible.

Introduction

"I love him. I know I love him. He's the best man I've ever met and I know he's right for me. But sometimes when we're together, I find myself screaming inside, 'Go away. You're suffocating me. I need breathing room!'"

Lisa suffers from emotional claustrophobia, the fear that another person, other people, or a certain situation can or will psychologically engulf, smother, or stifle her. Lisa describes her fear like this:

> I feel suffocated, trapped, like I might disappear entirely. Then I either go into a panic or feel dead inside, or sometimes I feel one way, then the other, and all I want to do is get away. I used to think it was the other person's fault—that they were doing or planning something against me. But I've observed myself enough times to know that most of the time, the fear is about me, not them. I can tell myself a million times that the other person isn't doing anything wrong and that I'm totally irrational to feel like I do, but that horrible feeling still comes over me. I try to make it go away, but it won't. Then I don't know what to do: stay or get away. Either way, I suffer. If I stay, I'm in agony. If I find a way out, I worry about hurting or alienating people or having them think I have a mental problem.

Lisa's fear of engulfment entraps her. She doesn't want to feel lonely or disconnected from others, but she doesn't want to feel suffocated either. She highly values having positive relations with friends and family members and being in an intimate relationship with someone special. Yet when she is near her friends or special love, her distress can be so great she feels the need to be alone.

Lisa experiences emotional claustrophobia primarily in her personal life rather than at work. Others experience it mainly at work. Still others, like Peter, might have it no matter where they are—in their living rooms with family or at meetings with coworkers and supervisors:

> *When that feeling hits me I want to bolt. If I'm at a party or family gathering, or even with my partner, I can usually find a way to escape. Then all I have to deal with is knowing that eventually I'm going to feel lonely.*
>
> *But at work, I have to worry about more than feeling lonely—my performance rating, possible promotion, and entire career are at stake. No matter how good I am at what I do, how will I ever get promoted if I can't tolerate certain kinds of interactions or meetings? I can pretend, of course, which is what I do all the time. But how long can I keep that up? I'm a great actor, but eventually someone is going to notice it's an act, if they haven't already.*

Rosa's fears of being smothered are sparked by her ability to feel her feelings on an unusually deep and intense level. She is an emotionally sensitive person who has the gift of being able to respond intuitively and emotionally to others and to various situations. This allows her to interact meaningfully with others and to make important contributions on the job. However, if a situation becomes too emotionally charged or she is confronted with several emotionally demanding situations in a short span of time, she becomes emotionally overwhelmed and has trouble thinking clearly. Her feeling of being smothered is heightened when these emotionally intense situations occur in closed spaces, such as movie theaters, concert halls, meeting rooms, or subways. Enclosed spaces are not the cause of Rosa's emotional claustrophobia, but sometimes they compound the problem. For Rosa, like others, being in confined quarters is an external reflection of an inner state of being of feeling confined or trapped by the flood of emotions experienced internally.

At some point, Peter, Lisa, and Rosa all decided that they were tired of being held hostage by their fear of engulfment and that they had sacrificed too much of their personal and professional lives to it. Swallowing their pride, they sought professional help.

In counseling, they learned that their fear of suffocation was rooted—in part—in prior experiences where they were unable to or did not know how to set limits on others or how to define what they were able to do or give in a certain situation. They were also relieved to discover that sometimes their fear of being suffocated by another person or situation had little to do with themselves or their past. Rather, their fear was an intuitive and accurate response to situations or persons who were overly demanding or who, given enough time and opportunity, could cause almost anyone to fear being coerced into sacrificing their heart, mind, pocketbook, or soul against their will.

In therapy, they uncovered and examined the origins and roots of their fear of being smothered. They also found means of managing it by anticipating it and practicing certain coping skills. These coping skills also helped them deal with aggressive and manipulative persons. As a result of their many efforts, Peter, Rosa, and Lisa became—and felt—increasingly stronger. They found that by working on their fear of engulfment they were able to totally eliminate this fear in certain situations. In other situations the fear persisted, yet even in these situations they were less worried about their fear and they had constructive ways of managing it so that it did not manage or dominate their lives.

Emotional Claustrophobia: A Common Dilemma

If you experience emotional claustrophobia, take comfort that fear of engulfment is not a psychiatric diagnosis. People with histories of depression, panic attacks, or anxiety or panic disorder may tend to experience this fear more frequently than others, but emotional claustrophobia can also affect people who don't have any diagnosable disorders.

Our society puts a premium on personal pride and self-assurance (rather than humility or loyalty to a group). It isn't fashionable or admirable to be afraid or insecure. To admit to being fearful is almost an admission of inferiority and abnormality. This is especially the case for men who, according to the traditional male stereotype, are generally expected to be self-confident no matter what the situation. However, in today's world of changing sex roles, many women, especially those in professional positions, are as hesitant as men to admit or reveal fears or insecurities.

You may fear being suffocated in only one relationship, in one type of relationship, or in many. You may experience emotional claustrophobia only with certain people, such as family members, friends, or sexual partners. Or you may experience it only in work or work-related settings; in interactions with people in community, religious, artistic, political, or special interest associations; or in specific situations, such as being presented with a project or commitment.

Whether you experience this fear with one person, or with many, in just a few situations, or in many, this fear can pose a formidable drain on your time, energy, and emotions.

Costs of Emotional Claustrophobia

Emotional claustrophobia is dehabilitating in and of itself, but it can also lead to the development of additional fears. For example, when you suffer from the fear of engulfment you might also develop fear about how you are perceived by others when you experience this fear. Do you shut down emotionally as the result of this fear? If so, do you then wonder if others might think you are cold, unfeeling, or antisocial?

Do you have trouble concentrating, remembering, or completing a task or project as a result of this fear? If so, do you worry that others might think you are incompetent, inept, or even stupid?

Like all fears, the fear of engulfment has a physical or bodily component. Does the anxiety you experience cause you to perspire, shake, or tremble? Do you then fear that others will call you "hysterical," "overreactive," "crazy," or "emotionally unstable"? If interacting with others is an important part of your job or profession, such fears about how you might be perceived can be especially strong and can serve to increase your daily levels of stress and anxiety. For example, if you are a salesperson or teacher, your fear of engulfment may interfere more noticeably with your occupation than if you are a computer programmer. However, regardless of what type of work you do you will be dealing with people, and the fear of being suffocated can definitely diminish your work abilities.

Like all fears, fear of engulfment does not lead only to a state of high anxiety and stress, but to anxiety's twin: numbing or emotionally shutting down. Whether you tend to become highly anxious or somewhat numb or "frozen," once the fear arises within you, your ability to rationally assess your options and make a good decision about a course of action will be crippled. You may have difficulties deciding what to do next, how to respond to the other person, or how to proceed with the situation or task at hand.

Fear of being stifled by certain people or situations can leave you feeling helpless, powerless, and extremely insecure. It can pose a formidable barrier to your personal and vocational functioning and happiness.

If you've decided that you're tired of being held hostage by your emotional claustrophobia and that you've already sacrificed too much of your personal or professional life to this fear, then this book may be for you. Perhaps you have fantasized about being able to handle situations, such as important staff meetings at work or critical family conferences, without feeling like you need to flee due to your fear of engulfment.

On the other hand, in the area of relationships, you may fear that if you take steps to minimize your fear of being smothered, you will threaten or lose relationships which are important to you. "How can I choose between taking care of myself and taking care of the relationships I value in my life?" you might wonder. This book is about both—how to deal with your fear of being suffocated in a relationship as well as how to keep, if not strengthen, that relationship as well.

Causes of Emotional Claustrophobia

Your fear of engulfment can be the result of both external and internal factors. Externally, if you are confronted with a person who actually does want to consume all or parts of your life, being afraid of being bulldozed by this individual is entirely appropriate. But if you experience this fear even with people who are not especially demanding, invasive, or potentially aggressive, then your fear of being smothered probably arises primarily from your past experiences. Internally, your fear of engulfment may be based on the difficulties and conflicts you have about not being able to refuse another person or organization's requests. As a result, you may fear, and often legitimately so, that you will overgive emotionally, financially, sexually, or otherwise. So much might be expected and taken from you, you may fear you'll cease to exist.

Fears of being smothered often involve fears of not being able to stand up for yourself and that, as a result, you may allow yourself to be humiliated or abused. This doesn't mean you are weak or inadequate, but rather that you were inadequately taught how to interact with others in a way that was self-respectful as well as respectful of others. Or perhaps certain teachings you were exposed to did not give you permission to stand up for yourself without feeling guilty. Alternatively, your fear of engulfment could be rooted, at least in part, in prior experiences where you were trapped in situations where it was emotionally or physically dangerous for you to stand up for yourself.

Some people fear being smothered in response to certain situations, rather than in response to a particular person or groups of people. However, fears relating to certain situations are almost always rooted in prior negative interactions with people. For example, if you experience fear of engulfment before beginning a book, course, or project, your fear can probably be traced back to a similar situation which involved at least one human being who caused you to fear being engulfed. The situation need not be identical to the one experienced in the past, but it needs to be similar enough to evoke feelings of helplessness, powerlessness, or confusion, which can lead to fears of being overtaken.

Suppose you experience fear of suffocation before beginning to read a novel. Such a fear could hearken back to any number of human interactions where you felt intimidated, overwhelmed, or inadequate. For instance, reading a novel may remind you of instances where you were scolded for "wasting time reading" by someone who wanted you to do something else or who was angry at you or jealous of you. Or perhaps you were told you were "too stupid" to understand or "too lazy" to finish the book. If reading novels was your way of escaping from someone who was possessive or overly demanding or from other unhappy realities, picking up a novel may be associated with all the pain and anguish of these interpersonal situations.

Many people experience a fear of being smothered on the job, when they are asked to complete a project or participate in a group decision. These types of situations can bring to the fore any history of emotional abuse or other negative interactions you've ever had about your ability to achieve or perform competently. They can also bring to the fore any unresolved issues about how decisions were made in your family of origin (when you were relatively small and powerless) or about how decisions were made during a life-changing event (such as the severe illness of a loved one or a trauma, such as a vehicular accident or assault). Victims of family violence or political torture frequently experience some terror in small or closed rooms. Their fear of suffocation in small spaces or confined quarters, such as automobiles, boats, or other vehicles, may have originated in life-threatening experiences where they were held captive in confined quarters. In sum, most often situational fears of engulfment can be traced back to a situation involving human beings.

Fears of being psychologically stifled frequently occur in situations that are new and where you have not had a chance to think about your needs and limitations. Under these conditions, you may not know what your boundaries are or how to set them. On the other hand, even if you know your boundaries, you may fear that you will not have the power to establish and enforce them because the other person won't respect or honor them. In such cases, you may legitimately fear that the other person will require of you more than you want or can give. This can make you feel as if you will be obliterated by that person.

Empowerment and the Empowerment Process

Empowerment doesn't mean eliminating the fear, but instead learning to understand it and finding ways of managing it. Just reading and completing the exercises in this or other self-help books or attending a few therapy sessions will not make your fear disappear quickly and painlessly. However, by confronting your fear directly and taking certain action steps to better understand and manage it, your fear of engulfment can diminish in intensity and frequency, and in the level of distress it creates in your life.

When you first begin this book you may feel relieved as you discover that you are not alone, that many others suffer from emotional claustrophobia. You may feel elated to learn that you are not crazy, that fear of being smothered is a normal reaction to certain very common life situations, especially situations involving exploitation or overly demanding or psychologically disturbed people.

But as you progress in your efforts, you can expect to experience two uncomfortable stages: the first is at the beginning of the empowerment process; the second is after you have made significant progress. At the very beginning, there is a sense of relief that comes from realizing that your problem has a name, is experienced by others, and can be remedied. However, as the feelings and memories which underlie your fear rise to the surface, you may feel panicky or overwhelmed. In addition to your fear of being smothered by personal, social, or work relationships, you may begin to fear being absorbed, overwhelmed, or even obliterated by your own emotions.

Some people report feeling as if they are choking, drowning, or "falling apart." Others become highly anxious and experience rapid heart rates, intense perspiration, and other signs of stress. This initial stage of healing has been called the "emergency stage" (Bass and Davis 1988). It may seem like it gets worse before it gets better when you begin the process of empowering yourself, especially if your fear of engulfment is rooted in painful or traumatic experiences.

During this initial stage of emotional awareness, you may even experience an increase, rather than a decrease, in your fear of engulfment. But it won't last forever. Nevertheless, because the fear of engulfment tends to intensify during this initial stage of growing awareness, it is critical that you have or consider obtaining the support of a qualified mental health professional, a support group, or a physician.

The Crisis of Recovery

You may also need support during the second point in the therapeutic progress: after you have made so much progress that you are truly ready to change. Even though you have worked very hard to acquire the understanding and techniques to be able to free yourself from some of your emotional claustrophobia, the prospect of such a change may be terrifying to you. It is at this point, when you are on the brink of freedom from certain fears that a new fear, fear of the unknown, of a life unrestricted by fear of being smothered, may overtake you and cause you to revert back to your old patterns.

Recovery, like any form of change, is also a form of death. Emotional claustrophobia is part of you and your identity. Even though you may consider it a highly undesirable part of your life, as it starts to diminish in importance, you may go through the stages of grief identified by Elisabeth Kubler-Ross (1969), commonly associated with the loss of a loved one or one's own process of dying. These stages include denial or shock, depression, bargaining, anger, and acceptance. The grieving process for a lost part of the self can be just as agonizing and painful as grieving the loss of a loved one, especially when the symptom you are recovering from was a form of connection or symbolic of a connection with a person or value that was an important part of your life.

Should you become afraid of what you've worked so hard to achieve or begin to grieve about how you have changed, do not be ashamed. It's only human to prefer the familiar to the unfamiliar, even if the familiar has been the cause of considerable misery. It's important to share any sense of loss you feel with someone understanding, talk about your fears of finally breaking free, and examine them as carefully as you will have examined your fear of engulfment.

Is This Book for You?

This book can help you if:

- you feel too overwhelmed to make a commitment to a person or difficult project or job.

- you dread family gatherings, social events, or work-related events because they stifle or deaden you.

- you fear that having close friendships, family ties, or active social or romantic relationships will rob you of your identity.

- when confronted with demanding people or situations, you feel your only options are to flee or to forget your needs beliefs and just do what others expect.

- you feel suffocated by certain people or situations but don't know why or what you can do about it.

- you feel anxious and guilty about feeling suffocated by these people or situations.

- you have given up valuable personal, social, and professional opportunities because of your fear of being smothered by certain people or situations.

Cautions

Many people who suffer from fear of engulfment feel their lives are quite satisfactory and relatively free of deep-rooted sorrows— with one possible exception: a persistent or intermittent fear of being overwhelmed by another person or situation. However, fear of engulfment is also commonly experienced by people who suffer from a panic, anxiety, or dissociative disorder; from clinical depression or manic-depressive illness; or from a post-traumatic reaction, such as post-traumatic stress disorder. If you suffer from one of these or another coexisting psychiatric diagnosis, remember that you will need to work separately on these issues.

If your fear of suffocation is related to having been abused, terrorized, or otherwise traumatized, then dealing with fear of engulfment will necessarily involve examining your past traumas. If you have a trauma history or are currently suffering from a major psychiatric disorder, it is recommended that you use this book under the supervision of a qualified mental health professional. You will also need professional care if you are experiencing severe life crises or are actively abusing alcohol, drugs, or food. This book is a useful adjunct to professional help, not a substitute for it.

The exercises and techniques presented in this book have been used by many mental health professionals and are safe for most people. Any exceptions will be clearly noted in the text. For example, this book is not suitable for individuals with DID (dissociative identity disorder, formerly known as multiple personality disorder) and is not a guide for survivors of family violence or sexual assault in confronting their abusers. The issue of confronting a former assailant needs careful consideration and planning. Professional guidance is recommended. Books for the layperson on this topic are listed in the appendix.

Furthermore, if while reading this book, you develop any of the following symptoms (or any other symptoms which disturb you), stop reading this book and seek professional help immediately: hyperventilation, uncontrollable shaking, or irregular heartbeat; suicidal or homicidal thoughts or impulses; feeling that you are losing touch with reality, even temporarily; having hallucinations or extremely vivid flashbacks of certain traumatic events; feeling disoriented, "spaced out," unreal, or as if you might be losing control; extreme nausea, diarrhea, hemorrhaging, or other physical problems, including intense, new, or unexplained pain or an increase in symptoms of a preexisting medical problem; severe memory problems or anxiety; self-mutilation or the desire to self-mutilate; or self-destructive behavior such as alcohol or drug abuse, self-induced vomiting, or compulsive gambling or overspending.

The appendix provides suggestions for further reading on managing anxiety disorders, depression, or past traumas.

How to Use This Book

Simply reading this book will not produce significant change. You need to complete the writing assignments if you expect to make gains in understanding and managing your fear of being smothered. Any type of change or growth requires time, energy, and concentration. If fear of engulfment was not already consuming more of your time, energy, and concentration than you are comfortable with, you probably would not have purchased this book in the first place. In the short run, completing the exercises in this book will definitely take up some of your time. In the long run, however, if you learn to manage your fear of engulfment, you will be saving the time you now spend dreading encounters that give rise to this fear and the time spent recuperating from such encounters.

Despite your sincere desire to deal with your emotional claustrophobia, you may still lack the motivation to complete the writing assignments. If this is the case, you may want to seek support for your efforts, such as the the help of a mental health professional or friend. Another option is making a commitment to another person that you will make a "date" with yourself to work on your fear of engulfment.

Read this book slowly and work on the written exercises at your own pace. Set a time limit on the amount of writing you do. Try not to write more than thirty minutes at one time. There may be occasions when you want to write more. Feel free to do so, but stop at the first sign of becoming overwhelmed, anxious, or "tuned out."

It is fine to skip around while reading this book, but the exercises are presented in a logical order. One exercise builds on the next. If you do not adhere to the sequence of written exercises, you will lose some of the benefits of completing the writing assignments. In fact, some of the written work will be impossible to complete without having replied to previous writing assignments.

How This Book Is Organized

Chapters 1 and 2 describe some of the most common causes of fear of engulfment. Some of these causes may be relevant to you, others may not. You can skip over the causes which do not pertain to you and focus on those which seem pertinent to your life.

In chapter 1, "Did Your Family Contribute?", causes of fear of engulfment which originate in childhood or in one's family of origin are examined. These include the anger, jealousy, intrusiveness, or unrealistic expectations of a parent or caregiver and any physical, sexual, and emotional abuse by a parent or caregiver. Other possible causes of fear of engulfment described in this chapter are: being stifled by overly close relationships with a family member, being used as a pawn in family conflicts, and living with a family member who was traumatized or severely stressed. Self-assessment exercises are provided for each of these causes to help you determine which of these causes is relevant to you and assess their impact on your life.

In chapter 2, "Did People or Events Outside Your Family Contribute?", additional causes of fear of engulfment are explored, such as harmful events or people outside your family; difficulties setting boundaries; experiences with extreme or rigid organizations and belief systems; the human emotions of anger, anxiety, and sexual arousal; and overpowering personalities. The self-assessment exercises in chapter 2 will help you determine which of these causes apply to you.

In chapter 3, you are guided in completing an Emotional Claustrophobia Inventory. Your first task will be to list as many fear of engulfment experiences as you can remember. From this list, you can select three experiences to examine in depth by describing what happened, the quality of the fear you experienced, your physical and bodily reactions to the fear, how you responded to the fear once it started, and how you talked to yourself during the incident. You will also be asked to try to identify what you were thinking and how and why you felt trapped during the incident, as well as the prices you pay for suffering from fear of engulfment.

In chapter 4, "Do Your Fears Belong to the Past or the Present?", you will identify the causes of your fear of engulfment in the three incidents you've selected for special attention, as well as consider which of these fears belong to the past and which belong to the present. Specific action steps are recommended if the causes of your fear of engulfment are related to problems with anger or anxiety management; child abuse or trauma; ongoing abuse or mistreatment; overbearing or manipulative personalities; or sexual arousal.

Chapter 5, "Managing Your Anxiety," describes various methods of self-soothing and self-calming. These include deep breathing, abdominal breathing, calming breathing, progressive muscle relaxation, eye relaxation, physical exercise, and creating a safe place.

In chapter 6, "Taking Charge of Your Mind: Evaluating Your Beliefs," you will try to uncover self-defeating beliefs which contribute to your fear of engulfment and sort out helpful and true beliefs from those that are no longer true or helpful. The next step is to begin to create new, more accurate, and more desirable beliefs.

In chapter 7, "Making a Plan," you will map out a way of handling fearful situations. This will involve visualizing an instance of fear and then visualizing the same instance again with a desirable outcome. Your plan for making the desirable outcome a reality will involve identifying your goals for the situation and using your desired beliefs, rather than the old beliefs that helped to create your fear of engulfment. This chapter will also instruct you in the use of certain communication skills that are necessary to the success of your plan.

Chapter 8, "Living Your Plan," provides guidelines on how to encourage yourself once you have made the decision to try out your plan and how to evaluate its effectiveness in reducing your fear of being smothered by certain people or situations.

The Value of Writing about Painful Experiences

Research has shown that writing about painful or difficult experiences can be very helpful. Like being in group therapy, writing can help to boost your immune system and keep your body healthy (Pearlman 1994). Writing, like any form of expression, can be a healing activity. Writing about troubling experiences and the troubling aspects of your relationships helps you to see them more clearly and gives you a sense of mastery over your experiences. Once you put something down on paper, you may make connections you were not previously aware of and you may get in touch with feelings you haven't experienced before. You may start to grieve losses that you haven't grieved previously. Such grieving is painful in the short run, but it can be healing in the long run because unresolved grief is an obstacle to emotional growth. Also, getting in touch with your losses may be the beginning of being able to make plans and decisions for your future.

Questionnaires and Exercises: Keeping a Journal

Working through this book is a process. This means that you may need to reread, reevaluate, and expand on your work as you go along. For this reason, it will be helpful to keep a journal of all the writing exercises you do. If you already keep a personal diary, it's still best to make a separate journal for the work you do from this book.

Many chapters include either questionnaires or written exercises. The more honest and thorough you are in completing these exercises, the more you will learn about yourself and help yourself to change and heal. I recommend that you buy a three-ring binder, dividers, and loose-leaf paper. Since you will be asked to go back, reread, and add to the writing you have done for previous exercises, using a loose-leaf notebook will enable you to add sheets as necessary. You will also be asked to write on a number of specific relationships and topics, such as feeling betrayed or becoming numb. The dividers will make each topic distinct and easy to find later on.

A number of exercises have been provided with blank lines for you to begin the exercises while you are still reading. It is highly recommended, however, that you transfer your answers to the pages in your three-ring binder, both for the additional space to write complete answers and for the ease of finding them for review.

A Final Note

Because a relationship depends on the interaction between two persons there are no guarantees that the suggestions made here will completely transform your relationships. However, you can exert more control over how you act and what you say and do in a relationship. The response of the other person is not under your control, but you can do your best to communicate clearly and to protect yourself from being triggered into anger, grief, or depression.

Remember that this book is only a beginning guide for improving the quality of your relationships. No self-help book, regardless of its value, is a substitute for individual, couples, or family counseling.

Some of the writing exercises and suggestions may be helpful; others may not be. What helps one person may not help another. If a particular writing exercise does not apply to you or doesn't offer you insight or relief, this doesn't mean that you don't have the "right" answer or that you aren't trying hard enough. Trust your instincts, but remember that the point is to confront and alleviate your fears.

Part I

Understanding Emotional Claustrophobia

Chapter 1

Did Your Family Contribute?

Fear of engulfment can have one cause or many. It can stem from having been trapped in an overbearing relationship or from a victimization experience where you were assaulted or exploited.

Emotional claustrophobia can also stem from growing up in a home where someone else survived a trauma or an extremely stressful set of life circumstances. Young children tend to be like sponges: they are biologically wired to be responsive to their parents' feelings. Whether you were raised by your biological parents or by stepparents, grandparents, foster parents, or other caretakers, as a child you were attuned to the emotions of the adults responsible for your care.

If either your mother, father, or another adult in your family was subject to severe trauma or stress, his or her feelings of anger, pain, and grief were undoubtedly and justifiably intense. These feelings can be so strong they are almost unbearable to adults, much less a child. Any child exposed to such strong emotions could easily come to feel engulfed by them. Then, as an adult, that child could easily feel engulfed by the strong emotions of others or by persons or situations which are reminiscent of one's parents or the parent's trauma or stress.

Difficulties setting boundaries is another major source of emotional claustrophobia. Any of the experiences previously discussed can easily lead to difficulties setting limits on your own activities or in your relationships. Feeling conflicted or unable to establish personal boundaries can also be the result of growing up with parents or other important people who had poor boundaries of their own or who rejected, ridiculed, or otherwise punished you when you tried to assert your legitimate needs and wants. You may also find yourself struggling with the issue of boundaries if you grew up in a home where extreme and conflicting demands were placed upon you or if you were involved with religious, political, or social organizations that demanded most of your time and attention.

On the other hand, your fear of being smothered may have little to do with the past, but may be an accurate response to people in your life today who are engulfing (or potentially engulfing) because they have intense negative or positive energies or are skilled at emotionally manipulating others. Fear of engulfment can also be a reflection of your difficulties with certain emotions, such as anger, sexual desire, or anxiety. Although usually pleasurable, sexual desire can be problematic when people feel guilty about their desire or fear that their desire is uncontrollable and might lead them into self-destructive sexual behavior. Sexual desire is also problematic when it conflicts with personal, moral, or religious standards, or when it is experienced in reaction to someone toward whom there are also strong negative feelings.

In this chapter, causes of fear of engulfment that can be directly traced to your family of origin or early childhood will be explored more fully. The next chapter will explore additional possible causes of this fear. In both chapters you will be asked to complete writing exercises designed to help you identify possible sources of your fear of engulfment.

Answer these questions as honestly and completely as you can. If a question does not apply to you, skip it and proceed to the next question. You will also be asked to observe and write about your emotional reactions to these questions. Your reactions might provide valuable clues to how you responded in the past to the situations you are writing about.

Knowledge is power. Understanding the origins of your fear is the first step toward mastering it.

Parents and Caregivers

As a child, you were so small physically and so dependent on your caregivers that they almost consumed your life. Your early years were spent enveloped in their arms and in their home. Their emotions surrounded you and you inevitably responded to their emotional state, as they did to yours. In many ways, you were at the mercy of their care and wishes. When you were very young (unless you were very unusual) you instinctively put aside your wants and needs and followed your caretakers' wishes. Since your survival depended on their goodwill, going against them would have been a very dangerous proposition.

Given the difference in size and power between children and their caregivers, it would be quite natural for children to sometimes fear that one of their caregivers might harm or even kill them. This is especially the case if one or more of the caregivers is or was violent or abusive. However, fear of engulfment is about feeling suffocated or smothered, not about being beaten or killed.

The idea of parents suffocating or overwhelming their children can be found in many primitive myths. In these myths, parents do not kill their child for nourishment: they swallow the child whole and the child stays alive in them, engulfed in their body. One view of these myths is that they express the young child's fear of being taken over physically or psychologically by the presence and expectations of the physically stronger and more mentally competent parent. This fear can be seen as entirely normal given the small size, undeveloped mental capacities, and emotional and physical dependency of the child on the parent.

Parental Jealousy and Hostility

Another interpretation of myths where parents engulf their children is that some parents are jealous of their child's vitality, innocence, or beauty and engulf the child in order to incorporate the child's qualities within themselves. Still another interpretation is that the parent stifles the child's growth because the parent fears the child will grow to become a sexual rival or undermine the parent's power.

Even the most caring and responsible caregivers may experience flickers of jealousy toward their child and wish to incorporate aspects of their child which they have lost to age, disease, time, or other factors. Even caregivers with a considerable amount of self-assurance can sometimes resent the attention a child receives and a child's potential power in the family.

In stepfamilies, blended families, or foster-care families, jealousies between family members are to be expected at first, as biologically unrelated individuals take on the challenge of coming together as one unit. If you grew up in a home where one or more of your caretakers was not biologically related to you, and the initial normal jealousy lasted a long time or grew stronger over time, then you might have been the target of jealousy not only from one or more adult caretakers, but of one or more of their biological children or biological adult relatives, who may or may not have approved of the adoption, marriage, or foster-care arrangement.

If one of your caretakers had momentary feelings of jealousy toward you, you might have picked up on those feelings and felt threatened by them. This jealousy might have made you fear that this individual would not take care of you or would abandon you or that they would convince those most responsible for your care to reject or mistreat you. As a result, you may have developed a transitory fear of being smothered that reflected these negative feelings toward you.

However, if for the most part your caretakers acted appropriately and rarely or never acted on jealous or hostile feelings toward you, or if they basically ignored the attempts of others to reject or harm you, then it is highly unlikely that your current fear of engulfment can be traced to this source. Only if your caretaker's feelings of hostility and jealousy toward you were strong and persistent and led to actions which inhibited or twisted your growth as a child could they be considered potential sources of your fear of being smothered.

If it was the negative feelings of a family member which contributed to the development of your emotional claustrophobia, then whenever you find yourself in situations with people who remind you of your caretakers, such as other authority figures, or when you're with people whom you feel have power over you (as your parents or caretakers once did), you may fear being engulfed by these persons in your life today much like you feared being engulfed by a caregiver in the past. As a child, you had few defenses against such strong negative feelings directed at you by important others. Today, as an adult, you can develop such defenses, which is one of the purposes of this book.

Physical and Sexual Abuse

Definitions of what constitutes abuse and battering vary. However, generally battering is any violation of a person's integrity, personal space, mind, or body, within an intimate, family, or otherwise emotionally bonded relationship where the victim feels that the abuser is capable of maiming or killing him or her.

Abusers often construct a rather complete trap for their victims. Physical violence is only one aspect of this trap, but it is the aspect that enforces the social, economic, psychological, and sexual control the abuser wields over the victim.

The physical aspects of abuse include pushing, shoving, holding victims down or locking them in the house to prevent them from leaving, slapping, biting, kicking, choking, hitting, punching, throwing things at the victim, abandoning the victims in dangerous places, raping, making threats of harm, or driving recklessly. Abuse also includes refusing to help the sick, injured, or pregnant.

The social aspects of abuse include denying the victims the freedom to choose their friends; attempting to isolate victims from others (including family members); verbally humiliating the victim before, during, or after social events; and refusing to let the victims attend social functions they want or need to attend. The abuser may use social events as a weapon by delaying the victim's commitment to attend, making attendance a reward for compliance to demands, and displaying unpredictable behavior during social events.

The economic aspect of abuse can include controlling family finances, including the victim's earnings; controlling whether or not the victim works and his or her choice of a job; harrassing the victim at work; calling the victim's employers and coworkers to make threats or demean the victim; and controlling the money for healthcare, children's needs, and family obligations and events (such as holidays, phone calls, gift-giving, visits, and attendance at funerals, weddings, or other religious events).

Emotional abuse includes ignoring the victim's feelings; ridiculing or insulting a group the victim belongs to (his or her gender, religion, sexual orientation, racial or ethnic background, profession, etc.); insulting the victim's cherished beliefs; withholding approval or affection as a means of punishing; criticizing or calling the victim names; shouting at victim; insulting his or her family or friends; refusing to socialize with the victim; humiliating him or her; refusing to work or share money; punishing the children when the abuser is mad at the victim; threatening to kidnap the children if the victim leaves; abusing pets to hurt the victim; manipulating him or her with lies and contradictions; and making all or most of the decisions about the victim's life.

Emotional abuse is so important it constitutes a category of abuse in itself, apart from physical or sexual abuse, and is dealt with as such in the following section. However, it is also a part of battering and most victims of physical or sexual abuse state that the emotional abuse they endured was almost as hurtful, if not more hurtful, than the actual physical or sexual violence they suffered.

Sexual abuse includes not only forced sexual activity, but making demeaning remarks about victims' gender or sexual desirability;

insisting that they dress in a more sexual way than they want; minimizing the importance of their feelings about sex; criticizing them sexually; insisting on unwanted sex acts; withholding sex and affection; insisting on unwanted touching; publicly showing interest in other potential sex partners; or having affairs or talking about having affairs with others after promising monogamy.

Abusers often label their abusiveness as a type of love or necessary discipline. But love is not supposed to hurt and all abuse, no matter how disguised as love, is not loving and involves hostility.

Regardless of the specifics of your history, being trapped in an abusive home or an abusive relationship is by definition a suffocating experience. During the actual moments of abuse, the abuse engulfed you emotionally and physically, if not sexually as well. Some of your fears of certain situations, such as making decisions or commitments or being in certain locations, types of rooms, and types of gatherings, may be related to your abuse history.

Abuse is all-encompassing. It affects the victim not only during the time it is happening, but also afterward, and it colors almost every aspect of family life. In many cases, the abuser was not only physically or sexually harmful, but also dominated, or tried to dominate, the victim's social life, spiritual life, healthcare and education, and relationships with others.

If you distanced yourself emotionally or put yourself in a trance or state of numbness during the abuse, you might not have *felt* engulfed, but you were. Numbness was not a sign that you were unaffected, but rather than you were defending yourself against overwhelming pain and stress.

Self Assessment: Physical and Sexual Abuse

On a fresh piece of paper in your journal, write the title "Physical and Sexual Abuse" and answer the following questions to the best of your ability.

1. Were you physically or sexually abused by a parent, caregiver, sibling, or other family member?

Abusers often label their abusiveness as a type of love or necessary discipline. But love is not supposed to hurt and all abuse, no matter how disguised as love, is not loving and certainly involves hostility.

Regardless of the specifics of your history, being trapped in an abusive home is by definition a suffocating experience. During the actual moments of abuse, the abuse engulfed you emotionally and physically. Some of your fears of certain situations—such as making decisions or commitments or being in certain locations, types of rooms, and types of gatherings—may be related to your abuse history.

Abuse is all-encompassing. It affects the victim not only during the time it is happening, but also afterwards, and it colors almost every aspect of family life. In many cases, the abuser was not only physically or sexually harmful, but also dominating in the victim's social life, spiritual life, healthcare, education, and relationships.

2. If you were abused, write three or four sentences about what it felt like to be overpowered by another person's emotional, sexual, or physical force. Write three or four more sentences about how the abuse has colored your self-esteem, family relationships, and relationships with peers.

3. Can you identify at least three ways that being abused was an engulfing experience, extending beyond the actual period of time you were being mistreated?

4. How does it feel to think about and write about your experiences with physical or sexual abuse? To what extent does thinking about this part of your life stimulate important emotions associated with that part of your past? If you felt overwhelmed or disoriented by your emotional response to this writing exercise, it's important to seek professional help.

Currently Abused

If you are currently being physically or sexually abused, get help. No amount of reading, therapy, or working on yourself will stop the abuse. You need professional and legal assistance. Contact your local social service agency, abused person's program, hospital, police department, or library to find resources available for those suffering from incest, partner abuse, child abuse, elder abuse, or other forms of family violence. Such forms of abuse are not only personal violations of the highest order, but legally punishable crimes. If you have difficulties locating help in your community or wish to do some reading about family abuse, consult the appendix for resources and recommended reading.

Emotional Abuse

Emotional abuse does not refer to a one-time incident of name-calling or ridicule: it refers to frequent or ongoing verbal abasement, rejection, and ridicule that results in feelings of humiliation and alienation. Another form of emotional abuse is being made into the family scapegoat. The family scapegoat is the person who is irrationally blamed for whatever goes wrong in the family, for example, illness, accident, failed romance, financial loss, or the wrongdoing of another family member. The family scapegoat is blamed for these or other problems, even though he or she alone could not possibly have had the power to cause any of these events. Stepchildren, adopted children, or foster-care children are more vulnerable to scapegoating and sibling rivalry, which exist in all homes to some extent but can be magnified by the presence of adopted or step-siblings.

Self-Assessment: Emotional Abuse

Title a fresh piece of paper in your journal "Emotional Abuse," and answer the following questions to the best of your ability:

Were you emotionally abused by a parent, caregiver, or family member? Who emotionally abused you? How often did the abuse occur? What was the content of the emotional abuse (i.e., What was said about you? Were you called stupid, ugly, evil, careless, worthless, crazy, dirty, or some other negative adjective)? As painful as it might be, make a list of the negative statements made about you. How often were you subjected to such humiliations: daily, weekly, only on occasion?

If you were scapegoated, who scapegoated you and what were you blamed for? Think of three or four negative situations for which you were blamed regardless of whether you did not wish for these situations to exist and could not have possibly caused them, or you *had* wished for them? Write three or four sentences about each of these events in your journal. Also indicate how often you were made the scapegoat. Then write five or six sentences about how being emotionally abused affected your feelings about yourself, your relationships with others, and your ability to love, work, and play.

Review what you have just written. Given the information before you, would you conclude that being emotionally abused was an overpowering experience that affected many aspects of your life?

Now think about the last few times you were given feedback or criticized. Write three or four sentences about how you reacted. Did you experience fear of engulfment at these times? What feelings do thinking and writing about being emotional abused bring to the fore? Remember that if you are experiencing severe distress you need to seek professional guidance.

Being emotionally abused or made into the family scapegoat means that a considerable about of negative energy and hostility was directed toward you by one or more family members. As a child, you had few defenses against such hostility, for it was coming from the very people on whom you depended for your survival and self-esteem. Consequently, being criticized as an adult, even when the criticism is mild or legitimate, may resurrect the emotional claustrophobia associated with your childhood pain.

In sum, emotional abuse, like physical and sexual abuse, is an overwhelming experience that can lay the groundwork for a subsequent fear of engulfment. If you were physically, sexually, or emotionally abused as a child and you currently suffer from fear of engulfment, it is quite probable that your current fear stems, at least in part, from these abusive experiences.

Was Your Privacy Invaded?

If you were abused in a family setting, the person who mistreated you may have been emotionally distant from you (except perhaps during the abuse). On the other hand, he or she may have been obsessively preoccupied with you to the point of trying to dominate your every move and the deepest levels of your psyche. Yet it is not necessary for a parent or caretaker to have been abusive in order to have invaded your privacy.

Emotionally immature or insecure family members tend to have problems establishing relationships with peers and engaging in activities that are meaningful to them. In an attempt to have human connection and life purpose, they may grab onto and try to absorb the life energy of another family member. The person they often turn to is a child, since children have fewer defenses and are emotionally and financially dependent on adults. The term "intrusive" is often used to refer to individuals who, in an attempt to fill the emptiness inside of themselves or to quell their many anxieties about living, physically and psychologically intrude on the life of another person (or other people). Intrusive adults can be characterized as emotional parasites: they feed off the feelings and life forces of other.

Intrusive adults are not necessarily physically or sexually abusive. Quite to the contrary, some may adore or almost worship the chosen child (or children). In some respects, they may truly love the child and contribute to the child's development. Their intrusiveness, however, is emotionally harmful. Furthermore, the fact that the parent or caretaker is not all bad or evil creates emotional confusion in the child.

If the parent is simply cruel, however, a child may feel anger toward that parent, and if the cruelty was severe enough, the child might even be able to denounce and reject that parent. But when a parent is both loving and giving, as well as demanding and intrusive, the child has mixed feelings. Having conflicting feelings toward a parent, such as both love and hate, both respect and resentment, makes it more difficult for the child to identify the parent's negative qualities and keeps the child bound to that parent for a longer time. It's easier to deal with having one dominant feeling toward another person than to have two strong and conflicting emotions about that individual.

Cultural Differences

What is considered intrusive in one culture may be considered normal in another. Cultural and religious groups differ widely on what is considered appropriate amounts of emotional and physical interaction and closeness. For example, many Americans view radio and television programs where people openly discuss their feelings and family problems. Yet such disclosures are unheard of in other societies, where sharing feelings and family matters with strangers is considered shameful and a betrayal of the family.

Another example is same-sex hand-holding, which (even between heterosexual males) is common in many parts of the Mediterranean and the Middle East, but rare in the U.S. If someone of the same sex wanted to walk down the street holding your hand in this country and you are not homosexual, you might consider that individual as being physically intrusive. On the other hand, if you were in Greece or Egypt, your refusal to hold hands, regardless of your sexual orientation, would be considered rude and insulting.

If your family or caregivers came from a culture or situation where there was limited housing space and many people were crowded into a few small rooms, it might not be considered intrusive for a family member, even a distant cousin, to come into your bedroom or personal space unannounced or uninvited, whereas in many as middle-class American families, such behavior would be construed intrusive. In many cultures, there is no concept of personal space or privacy. For example, there is no word that corresponds to the English word "privacy" in Russian and the very idea that having privacy is desirable is new to the culture (La Franiere 2000).

Within the U.S., there are important ethnic differences on what is considered "normal" closeness. For example, in general, White Anglo-Saxon Protestant groups tend to value individuality and emotional coolness. In contrast, Hispanic, Jewish, Arab, Slavic, Italian, and other groups of Mediterranean extraction tend to put a greater emphasis on interdependence among family members and on family loyalty, rather than on self-actualization and personal independence.

Also, among these groups, emotional expressiveness is generally more permitted than it is among Northern European groups.

Suppose your mother lives forty miles away and asks you to pick her up and take her to a family event. In some ethnic groups, such a request might be considered outlandish and intrusive. If you consent to your mother's request, your peers (or therapist) might see you as "overly dependent." On the other hand, if you are Italian, Greek, Jewish, or from certain African nations, such a request might not be considered intrusive at all, but quite normal. You might even be seen as selfish and disloyal to the family if you did not automatically agree to your mother's request. Also, if your mother didn't ask for you to pick her up and made other arrangements, you and other family members might assume your mother was angry with you and trying to insult you.

Trying to determine whether or not a specific behavior or expectation is intrusive or not becomes complicated if you are from a culture where it is normal and routine for family members to make heavy demands on one another or where personal space and privacy are not highly valued. Consider the following questions: Is this behavior generally accepted or considered "normal" given that person's cultural origins and cultural history? Would the cultural peers of that person consider the behavior intrusive or unusual, or would they consider it fairly routine? Would the cultural peers of that person act in similar ways without a second thought?

Assuming the person's behavior can be explained by cultural practice, you still need to consider whether the behavior exists in isolation or is part of a larger pattern of this particular person's behaviors that include acts that even people in his or her culture would consider extreme or exceptionally demanding? Even if the person's behavior is culturally acceptable and not part of a cluster of intrusive acts, the culturally accepted behavior may still be stifling to you. Even if a behavior is part of a cultural norm, and even if it isn't intended to be harmful to you, you may feel engulfed by it, and it can feel just as uncomfortable and intrusive.

If a specific action is intrusive to you, yet that action is widely practiced by others in your culture or the other person's culture, then you will be faced with an especially difficult dilemma. You will need to communicate to that individual that his or her actions are undesirable to you, even though, given that person's cultural background, the behavior is considered perfectly normal and ordinary. Trying to explain to that individual why their behavior is offensive to you may be complicated by the fact that person may see you as the deviant or offensive one for questioning what is generally accepted in his or her cultural background.

You, too, may feel deviant or disloyal to your cultural group if you find that a person's culturally sanctioned behavior is intrusive, offensive, or unacceptable to you. Just because a certain behavior is considered normal and permissible in a certain culture doesn't mean that it should be or is acceptable to you. In the first place, although many people in that culture seem to accept that behavior or custom, that doesn't mean they all actually like it. Some people who externally seem to have no problem with behaviors or cultural patterns you think are intrusive or suffocating may feel exactly as you do; however, they are hiding their discomfort, "grinning and bearing it," in order to feel accepted by others in the group. Secondly, among all groups, no matter how alike the people are, there are individual differences in interests, activity level, emotional reactivity, and emotional and spiritual needs.

Among immigrant and cultural groups, there are three patterns that can emerge in the process of adapting to the dominant culture. Some totally reject their ethnic background, adopting the language, clothing, religion, and lifestyle of the dominant culture, and consider their ethnic culture inferior. In essence, they divorce their heritage. Others cling to their roots more tightly, becoming rigid in the attempt to hold on to an ethnic identity that is difficult to maintain when the dominant culture has values that differ or conflict. All aspects of their culture, even parts that are not adaptive or helpful in a new environment, are considered sacred. And any deviation, even a legitimate one due to societal pressures or individual differences, is greeted with hostility and seen as a form of abandoning one's family and roots.

Still other people struggle with the issue of assimilating into the dominant society. They want to keep some aspects of the old culture, but not all. There are many decisions to be made and each one can be agonizing. There may be pressures from the older generation and from peers who have decided to stay as traditional as possible, to keep things the way they were. No individual exceptions are allowed.

If you are experiencing some of your culture's practices as intrusive and finding that when you try to create space for yourself, you are met with intense rejection and hostility, the great temptation may be to divorce your culture, as others have. In an attempt to free yourself from the particular cultural traditions that are suffocating you, you may find yourself considering disclaiming the entire culture.

Rejecting one's own culture can be a painful, devastating process, involving multiple losses. However, you may feel that your choice is to let your culture suffocate you or leave it altogether. It is at this point that you need to decide which aspects of the culture you enjoy and which are a source of strength and support to you, and which you find impede your personal growth or create a fear of engulfment. The clearer you can become about the specific actions or customs that cause your fear of engulfment, the more you can focus on setting limits on, or even totally abandoning, those specific aspects of your culture that cause you distress.

As is often said in twelve-step programs, "Take what you want and leave the rest." The idea is much harder to execute than it sounds. If you come from a family or a group that is determined to cling to the old ways no matter what, you may meet massive hostility when you attempt to change some aspect of the cultural norm. If your family or group within your cultural group is confused and conflicted about cultural change, then all the anxiety they have about what to change and how much to change may be projected onto you, when you are clear and firm about what you want and don't want from the culture. You can become the scapegoat for all their fears about change and all their fears about not changing.

For example, a recent survey of Latino-Americans (Goldstein and Suro 2000) found that 87 percent of first generation Latinos believed it was better for children to live in the parents' home until they married. Only 42 percent of non-Latinos agreed with this view. Hence if you are Latino and your first-generation parents oppose your leaving their home and establishing your own residence, their point of view is less likely to be an act of psychological intrusiveness on their part than if you are of Anglo-Saxon heritage. But that does not mean that if you are Hispanic you don't have the right to feel intruded upon when your first-generation parents insist that you will disgrace the family name by getting your own apartment.

In sum, you will need to take into account the cultural background of the individual you judge to be intrusive. An action that creates fear of engulfment in you may be routine for him or her. You cannot necessarily attribute a negative motive, such as jealousy or hostility, to someone who is behaving in a way consistent with his or her cultural heritage. Your challenge may then be to communicate with that person, not as someone who is maliciously trying to engulf or otherwise harm you, but as someone who doesn't understand that your needs are different from theirs, even though you may have a common cultural heritage. Depending on the culture, that individual may feel that you do not have the right to your individual needs, or that your separate needs are pathological or wrong or acts of disloyalty to the family or group. It is up to you, however, to decide what's best for you in lessening you emotional claustrophobia.

Self-Assessment: Intrusiveness

Title a fresh piece of paper in your journal "Intrusive Experiences" and answer the following questions to the best of your ability. As you reply, keep in mind what was or is considered normal for your ethnic or religious group. Is what you consider to be intrusive part of a cultural norm? If you have grown somewhat apart form that cultural group, you may now consider a certain behavior intrusive. However, in its original context, it may have been fairly common.

Therefore, if you are of Italian descent and your mother asks detailed questions about the food you eat, you cannot automatically assume that she is trying to control or suffocate you. Nevertheless, her behavior, even if culturally sanctioned, may still feel intrusive to you and you may decide that you want to take some action to limit her behavior. If her behavior is consistent with her cultural background, you would need to acknowledge that when you approach her about the issue. For example, you might say, "I know in Italy moms ask their children all about what they eat. That's a way moms show love. I know you love me, though, and it makes me uncomfortable when you ask me about what I eat. So even though I know you mean well, I don't want to have those kind of discussions anymore." If your mother doesn't respond to your request, use the guidelines in the later chapters of this book regarding setting personal boundaries and communicating them effectively to others.

Think back on your past. Did anyone in your family ever talk about wanting to "have you all to themselves" or "own your soul" or even "eat you up," and then follow through on such sentiments by frequently intruding on your life or trying to imitate you?

Did this individual invade your personal space by coming into your bedroom, playroom, or workroom to observe you, copy what you were doing or wearing, or ask you detailed questions about your thoughts, feelings, or activities? Can you identify at least three specific behaviors of this nature? How often did she or he intrude? Was it on a regular basis or only during a limited period of time?

For example, suppose the individual you suspect of being intrusive was your stepfather. When you were with others did he join in the conversation or activity without being invited, even when it was obvious that he was interrupting the bonding that was going on between you and the others? If so, how often did he behave in this manner? Looking back, does it seem to you that whenever you were being close or having fun with someone else, your stepfather intruded and tried to be a part of the interaction, and that your stepfather had difficulties initiating and sustaining human relationships on his own?

It's not necessarily intrusive for family members to sometimes include themselves in an ongoing activity, especially a celebration or party. However, if such behavior is not part of the norm in your religious or cultural group; if you clearly indicated that their presence was not desired; if they intruded upon ongoing activities many times and in many types of situations; and/or if their including themselves broke up the communication that was going on prior to their arrival, their actions could possibly be considered intrusive. This is especially the case if the activity was not appropriate for their age group or if they seemed incapable of maintaining personal, social, or professional involvements on their own.

For example, suppose you were raised by your grandmother, and that when you were a teenager and had a slumber party, your grandmother joined in on the party as if she was "one of the girls." While it may have been appropriate for her to spend time with your guests in order to be friendly and to supervise the party, it would not have been appropriate for her to put on nightclothes and participate in the small talk and giggling as if she were a teenager herself. Neither would it have been appropriate for her to ask your friends numerous personal questions and in other ways pry into their personal lives.

Such behavior suggests intrusiveness, especially if your grandmother had few friends or interests of her own. Any number of motives could have be operating. For example, she may have been trying to recapture her youth, trying to entertain herself, or jealously making sure that your primary affections remained with her instead of your friends.

A few isolated instances of such behavior is not grounds for assuming your grandmother (or any family member) was intrusive. However, if a particular family member repeatedly invaded your psychological space and you began to feel that individual was trying to take over you life (or sponging off of it) and then you spent considerable energy trying to figure out ways to sneak around or avoid that person so you could have some privacy or breathing room, it is probably fair to conclude that he or she was behaving in an intrusive manner.

As you record specific instances of intrusion in your journal, try to note the specific circumstances under which they occurred, for example, the physical setting, the time of day or year, or any specific event associated with this intrusiveness. Did the intrusions occur only at home, or did they also occur at school, at a workplace, in other people's homes, or at other locations? Were the intrusions associated with any specific holiday or with certain family events?

Were there particular aspects of your being which most interested the intrusive family member? Identify at least three of these, and write one or two sentences about each. When people in your life today comment or show interest in these aspects of your personality or life, do you experience emotional claustrophobia?

How did it feel to complete this exercise? Write two or three sentences about any strong feelings you had while thinking and writing about the intrusive individual. To what extent do you feel there is a connection between your current fear of engulfment and the intrusiveness you were subject to in the past?

Jealousy and Possessiveness

The family member who is jealous and possessive of you almost always acts in intrusive ways. Jealousy and possessiveness are also associated with abuse, since abusive individuals are typically insecure and like to keep tight control over their victims. Often they interpret any interest or relationship their victim has as a sign of betrayal or abandonment. For example, even a perfectly necessary and innocent relationship, such as a relationship with another family member or a friend from school, might have been the cause of a jealous fit or a retaliatory act.

Self-Assessment: Jealousy and Possessiveness

Title a fresh piece of paper in your journal, "Being the Target of Jealousy and Possessiveness" and answer the following questions to the best of your ability:

Looking back, was someone important in your life (especially a parent or influential adult) consistently or extremely jealous of you or possessive of your time and attentions? Can you identify at least three or four ways this person showed jealousy?

For example, did they *say* they were jealous? If so, what specifically did they say? Jealousy can be indicated by statements such as, "I wish I was as pretty (smart, strong, tall, musically inclined, artistic, athletic) as you," or "Your (father, mother, sister, brother, etc.) loves you more than they love me because you are so much (younger, prettier, etc.)." Possessiveness can be indicated by statements such as, "Don't forget, I'm your mother (father, brother, etc.), which makes me more important than any of these friends of yours," or "You owe me your time and dedication because if I hadn't adopted you/taken you in, you'd still be in that orphanage or with your lousy so-called parents."

If such statements were made only on occasion or in a light or jocular manner they may not be signs of profound jealousy. However, if such statements were accompanied by intense rage or emotional pain (such as tears, threats of suicide, or other threats) or by jealous actions (such as harming your body, stealing your property, spreading lies about you, or attacking your pets, property, friends, schoolwork), they can be considered sources of fear of engulfment, as well as other kinds of emotional pain.

In your journal, answer the following questions: What jealous and possessive comments were made about you? What jealous *acts* were committed against you? For example, if a family member was jealous of your academic or creative achievements, did he or she tear up your schoolwork or artwork, burn your report cards or certificates of recognition? In one case, a young man whose father was jealous of his writing abilities destroyed his son's computer. In another case, an older sister (who was responsible for her younger sister's care due to the absence of the parents) was jealous of her younger sister's swimming abilities. The older sister refused to buy the younger sister a swimming suit and forbid others from doing so as well.

If the individual was jealous of your appearance, did he or she prohibit you from purchasing attractive clothing or criticize your appearance? If the jealousy surrounded your relationship with another person, was the other person demeaned or were you made to feel guilt and shame about your relationship with this other person? For example, one man forbid his wife from driving her teenage daughter to social events on weekends. He insisted that his stepdaughter needed to learn to be "independent," however, his true motive was jealousy. He resented the close bond his wife had with her daughter and whenever his wife and her daughter were talking he would call his wife a "codependent retard" and his stepdaughter an "infantile weakling."

How frequently would the person in your life act in a possessive manner or make possessive demands? Weekly, daily, only on occasion, or only during a certain period of time?

Was he or she possessive with respect to most of the areas of your life, or only in a select few? Which specific aspects of your being gave rise to his or her jealousy? Your appearance, your position in the family (such as being first born or last born, or the boy or the girl), your talents or achievements, or the way you were being treated by another person (such as being the favorite of a parent or grandparent)?

Was the jealousy founded on reality or on distortions of reality, including delusions? For example, did one of your parents express jealousy of you for being more muscular, when, in fact, that parent was physically stronger than you? Did your sibling express jealousy of you for having more musical talent, when, in fact, you could barely play a tune? Did your mother express jealousy that your father loved you more than he loved her, when there was no evidence to support your mother's feeling? Did other family members or friends ever remark that a particular family member's jealousy of you was unfounded or extreme?

How did it feel to answer these questions? Did you experience any resentment, confusion, or fear, specifically a fear of engulfment? Are the feelings you had answering these questions similar to those you experienced while you were the target of someone's jealousy?

Were You Expected to Do or Be the Impossible?

Were you made to feel that your worth depended primarily or solely on your achievements or performance? Were you considered acceptable or lovable only if you measured up to a set of demanding standards, standards that were impossible for a child to live up to? For example, did your family expect you to master algebra equations when most children your age were still struggling with addition and subtraction? Were you expected to learn a second language quickly, fluently, and flawlessly? Was it mandatory for you to excel in sports or some other area when that area was not an area in which you were gifted or had interest?

Were the standards set for you too high not only for a child, but for most human beings? For example, were you expected to never get tired or sick, never complain about anything, or never tell a fib?

In such situations, you might have felt that if you didn't measure up to the expectations of your caretakers, you would be cast out of their hearts and abandoned. For a child, abandonment can mean both emotional and physical death.

It is natural for children to feel guilt and anxiety when they fail to meet the expectations of the individual or persons responsible for their care, but when these feelings become mixed with fears of being abandoned, the level of guilt and anxiety can skyrocket to such a level that guilt and anxiety dominate the psyche. Such feelings can easily lead to feelings of engulfment.

Adult demands can also become suffocating when the demands and expectations of one parent contradict those of another, as is often the case when parents separate or divorce. But even parents who remain together can put a child in this type of double bind. No matter which set of demands the child chooses to meet, the child runs the risk of alienating a cherished parent and incurring that parent's wrath.

Self-Assessment: Extreme or Conflicting Expectations

The purpose of this writing exercise is to help you bring out into the open the kinds of messages you were given during your formative years. You may have received these messages from parents or other significant persons who were directly involved in taking care of you.

Often people aren't aware of why they are experiencing suffocating feelings of guilt about a certain matter because they have not had the opportunity to examine early messages about how "good" people "should" be or act. If the consequences of not living up to such expectations included extreme shame or rejection to the point where you felt you wouldn't matter to your caregivers unless you measured up to these standards, then failure to meet these standards threatened your sense of being a valuable human being and of belonging to your family.

This problem of living up to parental standards is made worse if your parents strongly disagree on what is expected from you. The demands might not have been excessive, but if the demands contradicted one another, your anxiety level may have risen to such a high level that it affected your ability to think, learn, bond with others, and enjoy life.

This exercise will help you put into words the kind of values and actions you were expected to embody as a child. Later on, when you describe situations that cause you to experience fear of engulfment, you will refer back to your responses to this exercise in order to see how your fears about being humiliated or psychologically disinherited interact with parental expectations.

On a fresh piece of paper in your journal, write the heading, "Early Should Messages." Think of all the "shoulds" you learned about how you ought to be during the first twelve years of your life. On your paper, draw three columns. In the first column, list as many shoulds as you can remember. Include those shoulds you heard from your parents, neighbors, friends, family members, teachers, religious instructors, and the media.

In the second column, list the source of the should—where you learned it or who taught it to you. In the third column, describe what happened to you when you did not live up to this particular should. For example, were you verbally chastised, rejected, hit, or made to feel ashamed? Were you threatened with abandonment or some other punishment?

Look over your list of shoulds and notice if any of them contradict one another. If your parents separated or divorced, your list may contain many contradictions, since your parents may have separated partly because of the incompatibility of the shoulds they believed in. For example, suppose your mother told you it was okay to tell a white lie, but your father told you that any form of deception was a major sin. Or perhaps one of your caretakers gave you a double message. For instance, suppose the very same grandmother who told you that teenage sex was a disgrace to the family also emphasized that being sexually inactive meant you were abnormal and not a "real" man or woman.

On a fresh piece of paper, entitled, "Shoulds Contradictions," once again draw three columns. In the first column, list the discrepancies you found between all the things you were taught about how to behave, think, or feel. In the second column, describe how you coped with the contradictory shoulds you heard growing up. In the third column, describe what happened to you as the result of how you coped with the contradictory shoulds.

For example, if your mother taught you to fight bullies and your father taught you to turn the other cheek, perhaps you lied to your father when you fought back and then to your mother when you walked away from fights. Another possibility is that you didn't tell either of them how you responded to bullies and tried to carry the burden of being threatened at school all by yourself. Did you need to lie, steal, pretend, runaway, hurt yourself, or hurt animals or others as a result of the contradictory messages? Did you suffer from an intense fear of being abandoned or rejected or of being totally suffocated by the need to figure out a way to please two different sets of standards? If so, describe this in detail in your journal.

It is important to identify the early ways you responded to such pressures in order to see if you are responding with emotional claustrophobia today as you have in the past.

When Close Is Too Close

Everywhere my father went, I went. People used to call me his shadow because we were inseparable. Even in my twenties, I was so attached to my dad I didn't have my own personality. An invisible umbilical cord bound me to him.

But it was more than deep love between father and son. Our personalities were merged. I was him and he was me. Once, when I was twenty, I looked at him square in the face and thought I saw myself. I was so frightened I couldn't move. I was afraid being near him would totally suffocate me, even though I knew he would never purposely harm me.

I wanted to get away, but I was immobile. I felt I couldn't leave my dad, or he or I might die. As much as I resented my dad monopolizing my life, I couldn't imagine life without him. But I had to break away, or I would never have grown up.

It took ten years of therapy for me to emotionally separate from my dad and I'm still working on it. The guilt and terror I felt about separating from him and becoming my own person were enormous. We were both so emotionally dependent on each other. He enjoyed it—he thrived on it. But it was strangling me.

Bob and his father were too close. This doesn't mean that Bob loved his father too much or vice versa, for it is impossible to love anybody "too much." Being too close means that Bob and his father's personalities were almost merged and that Bob's individual growth was stifled by his relationship with his father. This type of relationship, where the personality and interests of one person are almost identical to those of the other and where one person (usually the younger or less powerful one) feels suffocated by the relationship, is called a symbiotic relationship.

In symbiotic relationships, the personalities are so similar it is almost impossible to distinguish one person from the other. Furthermore (and this is the critical aspect of symbiotic relationships) the development of one person is stunted by the needs of the other person. Symbiotic relationships between adults are suffocating, but symbiotic relationships between an adult and a child are even more suffocating, especially for the child (Kerr and Bowen 1988).

Symbiotic relationships originate in the normal, natural, and very much needed attachment between a primary caretaker and a newborn infant. This type of symbiosis is instinctive and is found not only among humans, but among many other mammals. In the first few years of life, children are so dependent on the mother and are so mentally and emotionally underdeveloped that they may even feel they are part of the mother's body. They may have trouble distinguishing their bodies from the body of their mother. According to several theories of child development, only as children approach the "terrible two's" do they begin to acquire a sense of having an identity separate from the mother or primary caretaker.

When a child is very young, it is natural and necessary for a child to have a symbiotic relationship with a parent or caretaker

(Kerr and Bowen 1988). However, in the normal progression of events, the young child gradually grows away from its mother or caregiver and gradually becomes an autonomous, independent adult. In some cases, this growth process is arrested and the symbiotic mother-child or caretaker-child attachment is prolonged into adult life. The symbiosis may persist because the child is disabled or needs special care for other reasons or because the parent and child are trapped in some terrible circumstances where they only have each other.

Perhaps the most damaging form of symbiosis occurs when parents turn to one of their children to meet their emotional needs for companionship, affirmation, and emotional support. Some parents also use their children for sexual purposes. When there is a divorce or death in the family, sometimes one of the children assumes some of the functions of the absent parent. For example, if the parent who used to do the cooking has died or left, one of the children may now assume the role of cook. If the parent who used to wash the car is now disabled, one of the children may take on that duty.

It is not uncommon, unnatural, or unhealthy for family members to help each other out or feel close to one another and turn to each other for increased comfort, companionship, or help after a death or loss in the family. But it is not healthy for separated, divorced, or bereaved parents to turn to one of their children for the emotional intimacy and support that they used to receive or had hoped to receive from their partner. When adults turn to a child for the emotional closeness that would otherwise come from an adult partner, that child can feel smothered by the needs of the adult and develop emotional claustrophobia as a result.

This discussion of symbiosis is not meant to imply that strong parent-child bonds or any other type of strong bonds are undesirable or psychologically unhealthy. Quite to the contrary, strong bonds with others, whether they be parents or friends, are not only psychologically necessary, but a major source of emotional strength and personal growth. In all close relationships there is tension between the needs of the individual for personal space and personal growth and the needs of the relationship. Furthermore, it is healthy to make compromises and personal adjustments for the sake of the relationship, provided they do not harm you.

However, in symbiotic relationships, individual development virtually ceases due to the demands of the relationship. The two personalities fuse so much that it's difficult to tell one person from the other and often the child feels stifled. He or she wants to grow beyond the confines of the relationship but is prohibited by feelings of obligation and love for the caregiver or by the sense that neither can survive emotionally without the other person.

In a state of fusion (or near fusion), each person is an emotional prisoner of the other person's behavior and emotions. In an adult-child symbiotic relationship, however, the child, due to immaturity and dependence, is much more a prisoner than the adult (Kerr and Bowen 1988). Children who have symbiotic relationships with a primary caregiver feel they cannot separate or be different from that adult without the adult revolting, falling apart, or punishing them by withdrawing love and support. In other words, the children feel they must choose between having a connection to the adult responsible for their care and protection and their own development.

Parent-child symbiosis is dramatically depicted in the Greek myth about Chronos, the king of the gods. In the myth, Chronos swallows his children whole as soon as they are born. They remain inside of him until, later on, Chronos is forced to regurgitate them. They emerge whole and unharmed.

Imagine Chronos's belly swollen with the bodies of his children. This is the very picture of parent-child symbiosis. During the time Chronos's children lived in their father's stomach, they grew physically and in other ways. But they could not grow beyond the confines of their father's body. Psychologically this myth depicts an engulfing parent and a symbiotic parent-child relationship. The parent does not kill or maim the child and the child continues to grow, even while consumed by the parent. However, the boundaries of the children's world and the horizons of their vision of themselves and of life are severely limited by their parent. Essentially the parent is strangling the child's development and the child comes to resent it.

Perhaps you had a parent, caregiver, teacher, spiritual leader, or some other authority figure who smothered you psychologically. You became a part of that person. Even though you were still a physically independent entity, other aspects of your life—perhaps including your emotions, thoughts, sexuality, etc.—developed under the shadow of that parent's being.

If you were in a symbiotic relationship as a child, you may fear that others in your life today will dominate or suffocate you the way a particular adult did when you were a child. As a result, you may shun all relationships, especially intimate ones, or you may tend to avoid relationships with people who are similar to the particular adult or person who overwhelmed your life.

Or perhaps you have become a "relationship nomad." You have close relationships, but when they start becoming even closer or more intense, you flee to another relationship. While physical escape is one way to handle fear of engulfment, another way is through internal withdrawing, or by starting arguments and conflicts.

For example, Amber had a symbiotic relationship with her mother. Amber's mother talked to Amber a lot and engaged her in long conversations almost daily. In grade school, Amber was forbidden from joining after-school activities because her mother wanted her home, ostensibly to help with housework, but in reality, for company and entertainment. In college, Amber had to come directly home from class and share her lecture notes with her mother, who then insisted on prolonged discussions of the lecture material. On those rare occasions when Amber visited with friends, her mother insisted on knowing all the details of her time with them.

Since Amber's mother demanded so much of Amber's time and psychic energy, Amber had little energy (or time) for relationships with peers, for studying, and for other interests. Amber's mother literally engulfed her life.

In order to escape her mother, Amber married the first man who proposed to her. He was also intrusive, demanding, and extremely possessive of her time. But because of her experience with her mother, Amber thought her husband's behavior was normal. She tolerated her husband until she experienced sufficient personal growth to realize that she was once again being suffocated. When her husband refused to give her breathing room, Amber left him.

Today Amber is free of intrusive, demanding people who want to consume every minute of her time and every ounce of her energy. But she is also very alone. If someone begins to talk with her about a topic she used to discuss with her mother, she immediately becomes hostile and shuts down. Amber has found that about ten minutes into such conversations, she begins to feel anger and resentment toward the person with whom she is talking and to have excruciating feelings of being trapped, the very same feelings she felt first with her mother and later with her husband.

In an effort to preserve her sense of self, Amber typically abruptly cuts off communication with the other person. Sometimes she tries to soften the blow by promising to contact him or her at a later point in time. She usually follows through, but out of a feeling of obligation, not a true desire to communicate. This was the same way she felt growing up: forced to communicate with her mother out a feeling of obligation—not desire. In truth, Amber wants to talk to others about a variety of topics, but because of the association between many kinds of conversations and her symbiotic history with her mother, Amber avoids such conversations at all costs.

Amber's fear of engulfment surrounding having conversations became a major impediment when she began dating. Amber was interested in marriage, but most of the marriage-minded men she met all wanted to have long talks—the same way her mother did. It was so difficult for Amber to overcome her past symbiotic relationship with her mother that for a while Amber abandoned her desire for marriage and became a "relationship nomad," going from man to man. Not until Amber began to address the impact of her symbiotic relationship with her mother was she able to tolerate the process of conversing and becoming emotionally intimate with others.

Self-Assessment: Symbiotic Relationships

Although symbiotic relationships usually arise between parents or other caregivers and children, they can also arise between siblings or between children and members of the extended family, such as grandparents, aunts, uncles, cousin, or even godparents. The critical element in distinguishing symbiotic relationships from other types of close relationships is not the amount of time spent together or the degree of caring, but whether or not you felt dependent upon the relationship while also strangulated by it.

Title a fresh piece of paper in your journal "Symbiotic Relationships" and answer the following questions as completely and honestly as you can. As you answer these questions, note your emotional state and write down a sentence or two about your reactions. Also, keep in mind what is considered normal and usual in your ethnic or religious group. For example, in some cultures first-born sons or daughters are expected to spend more time with their parents and assume more responsibility for the care of the parents in their old age. These cultural expectations certainly affect the perceived choices of first-born children, but this does not mean necessarily that their relationship with their parents is symbiotic.

Did you ever have a relationship with another person who was older or more powerful that met the following criteria:

- your personalities and interests were very similar;

- you both felt you needed each other a great deal;

- you were best friends despite the differences in your age and power; or

- you felt suffocated and stifled because all the energy you were putting into the relationship with that person was distracting you from your own growth and development?

The last criterion, that of feeling suffocated or stifled, is the most critical, for if you felt free to be yourself and grow in a relationship, the fact that you and the other person are similar, emotionally close, or need each other a great deal is not psychologically harmful. The harm lies in what Hannah Lerner (1985) calls "deselfing"—that is, in order to keep the relationship you have to give up too many of your beliefs and needs and have to continually adapt yourself to the other person's needs and desires at the expense of your own development.

1. How did you react when separated from this individual? Did you miss them some and experience some unease and confusion? Did you also experience relief from the burden of the relationship and joy at having the freedom to develop along your own lines? Did the older person or adult, however, do more than miss you? Did he or she lapse into a deep depression or become dysfunctional? Did he or she later tell you that it was impossible to cope or be happy without you? That no one could take your place? Did you feel guilt, as if you caused the other person's pain, but then feel angry that this individual had such an emotional hold on you that you felt you belonged to that person? Were you made to feel responsible for this individual's happiness, health, and fulfillment without knowing what to do to achieve these goals?

If you have answered "yes" to many or most of these questions, there is a high probability that you were involved in a symbiotic relationship with someone in your family. If you have answered "no" to most of these questions, then you can skip the remainder of this section and go on to the next section.

If you feel you were involved in a symbiotic relationship, answer the following questions in your journal. Try to write at least two or three sentences in reply to each question:

2. Who was that person? What was their relationship to you? In what ways were you the same? What personality traits, interests, or habits of theirs did you adopt as your own? If so, which ones? Did that person, in turn, adopt some of your traits, interests, or habits? If so, which ones? At the time, how did you feel when you saw that individual imitating you? How do you feel about this issue now? At the time, how did you feel about copying that individual's behavior? How do you feel about this issue now?

Did you feel pressured to invest a significant amount of your life energy in your relationship with that individual for fear that he or she might collapse if you invested significant portions of your life energy elsewhere? How much of your energy went into loving and feeling loved by that person?

Were their times when you experienced their anxiety, sadness, joy, and other feelings so much that you were unaware of your own emotions? Were there times you sacrificed your individuality, personal development, and needs for the sake of your relationship to that person? Did you feel you couldn't take care of yourself or manage your life without that person?

If that person developed a disorder or began repeating negative acts that interfered with their daily living, did you develop a similar disorder or begin to demonstrate negative behaviors similar to theirs? For example, if that person had an eating disorder, such as compulsive overeating or bulimia, did you develop a similar disorder or some other type of negative or self-destructive behavior? Or, when that person stopped his or her destructive behavior or seemed to be free of the disorder, did you begin to demonstrate the very same disorder or some other negative behavior yourself? For example, if your mother was an alcoholic or was addicted to illegal drugs, when she stopped drinking or using, did you begin to indulge in drinking or drugs?

Reread what you have written in your journal and then answer the following questions: During the time you had a symbiotic relationship with the individual you described above, how did you feel? Quite possibly, you had two sets of feelings—one positive, the other negative. On the positive side, you may have felt secure, loved, and special; on the negative side, trapped, resentful, or even furious. Write two or three sentences about each of the feelings you experienced.

Did you ever think of trying to escape the relationship (e.g. by running away from home, getting married, joining the military, or moving thousands of miles away)? Why did you want to escape the relationship? What prevented you from ending or leaving it? Be sure to write about not only your fears of being suffocated, but also your fears about separating from that person and no longer being merged with him or her.

What feelings are you having right now? Is fear of being smothered one of these feelings? Take a few minutes and reflect on the various emotions you have experienced while reading and responding to this section on being too close. Do some writing about these feelings. Are these feelings similar to the feelings you had while you were more closely involved in a symbiotic relationship?

Looking back, was it possible to change the relationship so that it allowed you breathing room? If not, why not? How do you feel when you look back on being stuck in that relationship? Do you see any connection between your current fears about being smothered and aspects of this (or another) symbiotic relationship?

If the person you had a symbiotic relationship with was a caregiver, you might want to consider the relationship between that person and his or her parents. How separate were they? Is/was your relationship with that caregiver similar to that person's relationship to one of his or her parents? In what ways are the caregiver and his or her parent similar or dependent? Is this the way you are or were similar or dependent to your caregiver? As you answer these questions, keep in mind that it is normal and healthy for children to be dependent on their parents and even to imitate their parents.

Were You Trapped in an Emotional Tug-of-War?

Were you trapped in an emotional tug-of-war between two people who mattered to you? When you were younger, did your parents or other adults in your family use you as an emotional shock absorber in their conflicts? As an adult, have you been an emotional pawn in a conflict between coworkers or superiors on the job? If you tried to please or side with one person, did you run the risk of being punished by another?

If your answer to any of these questions is "yes," then in psychological terms, you were triangulated. To be triangulated means to be used as an emotional pawn or a scapegoat in a relationship between two other people.

When Mary was seven, she observed her mother being beaten by a boyfriend. After her mother pressed charges and Mary was asked to testify, Mary became trapped in an emotional tug-of-war. On the one hand, Mary feared that if she testified as to what she saw, the boyfriend would retaliate against her mother (and herself) with more violence. On the other hand, if she didn't tell the truth, she would be betraying her mother. As a result of this and other similar experiences, Mary still experiences emotional claustrophobia in her adulthood whenever she is asked to make decisions. Even when the choices are relatively unimportant and have no major negative consequences, Mary feels suffocated, much as she did as a child when she was asked to select one of several unacceptable options.

Under ideal circumstances, when two people have a disagreement, they have an open and frank communication about their differences and try to reach a mutual understanding. This way of resolving conflicts assumes, however, that the two adults are able and willing to put their thoughts and feelings into words in ways that are self-respecting and respectful of the other person. It also assumes that they are capable of listening to one another and are willing to make some personal adjustments for the common good of the family or relationship (or the company or enterprise). If most adults were able to resolve their differences in this way, there would be less name-calling, yelling, or violence in families and much less injustice and violence in the world at large.

However, when people don't know how to put their anger into words that clearly communicate their anger but are not abusive of others, or when partners use each other as the scapegoat for their own unresolved issues or life pressures, conflicts can become verbally or physically abusive. Alternatively, there can be a stalemate where the issue of concern is simply not talked about, but is expressed indirectly in psychological symptoms, such as depression, addiction, or physical illness.

Some adults put their child in the middle. In this process of triangulation, parents draw another person into an ongoing battle. The two conflicting adults form an emotional triangle with a child. Instead of discussing and focusing on their problems, one or both of the parents discuss and focus on one or more of the children. The parents may argue about the child's behavior or dress, but these arguments are smoke screens for the parent's issues.

Suppose the parents argue hard and long about child-rearing issues, such as the amount of a child's allowance. If the arguments are long-lasting and severe, not because of the merits of the issue at hand and not because of concerns about the child, but because the disagreements are fueled with the anger, disappointment, and other types of emotional energy having to do with tensions in the marriage, then these parents are triangulating their child. The parents may legitimately disagree on a child-rearing issue, but the intensity of their disagreement and the degree of importance attached to the issue has more to do with unresolved conflicts between the parents than with different parenting philosophies.

Such arguments run rampant among separating or divorced couples, where children are used often as pawns and as means for the adults to vent their fury at one another. For example, Tawana, age five, used to call herself a Ping-Pong ball because she felt like she was being bounced between her parents during their ongoing custody dispute. Her father would tell her one thing; her mother another, and both parents expected her absolute loyalty. Tawana feared that if she didn't act loyal to a parent, that parent would abandon her. The problem was, she couldn't even pretend to be loyal to them both at the same time because they disagreed about almost everything.

Such emotional tugs-of-war can also occur among committed couples and their child. In either case, no matter what they do, triangulated children will incur the wrath of one of the two people whom they love and depend on the most.

Another type of triangulation occurs when one parent encourages the child to disregard the rules set by the other parent or turns to the child to meet some of his or her needs for companionship and emotional support that are not being provided by the other parent. A young child drawn into the parental conflict in this way may come to feel guilty for disobeying the other parent's rules or for having a secret understanding or relationship with one parent, but not the other. When the parents argue, that child may assume the blame for the parental strife.

For example, a man who is alienated from his wife but cannot or does not know how to constructively confront his wife about his marital disappointments may take his daughter to his company dinner instead of his wife. In this sense, the daughter has been triangulated. In the very same family, the mother may not feel free to tell her husband about her discontents with the marriage, but rather turn to one of the children as a confidant. The mother may turn to another sibling, or to the very same daughter to whom the father turned. In this case, the daughter is doubly triangulated and she absorbs the anxiety and stress of her parent's marriage and her parent's individual anxieties and personal pain.

While engulfed in the parental conflict, the triangulated child is not mastering a task, playing, or socializing with friends. The child's life is engulfed—and limited by—the parental drama, much like Chronos's children were limited by the size of his belly.

When parents come to physical blows, feelings of emotional claustrophobia can be tremendous. But even if the parents never become physically violent with each other, the child can sense the hidden anger between the parents and feel overwhelmed by the parental strife. When this child grows to maturity, he or she might experience fear of engulfment in emotionally intense relationships, especially if they involve hidden anger.

You may have escaped being triangulated in a conflict between two important adults during your childhood years only to find yourself triangulated today in conflicts between two people at work. Warring managers, competing employees, or other pairs of workers and supervisors who are in conflict but who, for a variety of reasons, do not confront each other directly, may triangulate or draw in another person to be the focus of attention.

For example, suppose the president of a company feels the work of one of the vice-presidents is of inferior quality, yet for political or other reasons, does not feel free to fire the vice-president. He would like to strike back at the vice-president directly, but dares not do so for fear of serious political repercussions. Instead, the president begins to complain about the vice-president's secretary: his work is incomplete and full of inaccuracies; he is absent too often due to his family responsibilities; he doesn't dress appropriately, etc. The vice-president defends his secretary, but at times, he agrees with the president that the secretary is incompetent, so as not to incur the president's wrath himself.

The controversy over the secretary is bogus: the real tension is between the president and the vice-president. This is an instance where the secretary has been triangulated into a conflict that has little to with the quality of his work and everything to do with the tension between his direct supervisor and the supervisor above him. If the secretary should quit due to the tension, the two warring parties would find some other person, or issue, to triangulate until they finally have the courage or opportunity to honestly discuss their differences. It would only be natural for the secretary to have acquired a fear of engulfment in his work relationships, especially with his superiors, after such an experience.

Self-Assessment for Triangulation

Title a fresh piece of paper in your journal "Triangulation" and answer the following questions to the best of your ability:

Looking back on your childhood, do you remember any instances where you might have been pulled into an emotional tug-of-war between adults in your family in any of the following ways:

1. Did one parent or caretaker urge you to break the rules set by another parent or important family member? For example, did one parent encourage you to sneak out of the house to meet your friends after the other parent had grounded you for a week?

2. Did you have to listen to one parent talk badly about the other? For example, for most of his junior high and high school years, when James came home from school, he was forced to listen to his mother complain about his father and to her descriptions of his verbal abusiveness and financial failures. On the other hand, when James's father drove him to soccer practice, James heard all about his mother's inadequacies from his father. Children growing up in single parent homes often are subject to hearing about the abuses and abandonment of the absent parent. Children whose parents

are undergoing divorce or separation are frequently exposed to tirades about the other parent's inadequacies or betrayals.

3. Did one of your caretakers turn to you to provide companionship and assistance which, according to the standards of your cultural and ethnic group, should have been provided by an adult partner?

4. Did one parent tell you "secrets" that you were supposed to keep from the other parent? For example, Randy's father violated his promise to his wife to limit his spending on new computer software. Every time he purchased new software, he asked Randy not to tell his mother and cover for him.

5. Did one (or both) parents treat you with special leniency that did not apply to your brothers or sisters?

6. Were all or most of the family's problems blamed on one of your behaviors or qualities? For example, was the family's unhappiness blamed on your eating disorder or addiction?

7. Did you feel you were in an inner circle with one of your caregivers and that other family members were in the "outer circle"? Who was in the inner circle? Who was in the outer circle? How did it make you feel?

8. Did either parent turn to you as the solution to his or her personal difficulties or as the solution to marital difficulties? For example, Marsha's parents regularly woke her up in the middle of the night in the midst of their fights and asked her to judge who was right and who was wrong. Even though Marsha was twelve years old, her mother didn't hesitate to shake her out of her sleep and say, "Wake up and talk some sense into your father."

9. Were there regular, predictable fights between your parents about some issue pertaining to you (e.g., your eating, spending, or dressing habits, your grades, your appearance, or your talents)? Were these fights more about some parental conflict than about you?

10. Did you ever feel uncomfortable in your family because you felt you had to take sides with one parent or the other (or another important person in the family)? Were you ever forced to take sides due to a divorce or custody battle?

If you can answer "yes" to any of these questions, write three or four sentences describing how you were drawn into an adult conflict. Then write another three or four sentences describing the effects you think being drawn into adult conflict had on you.

If you can, write an additional sentence or two about what you think was the underlying issue between the two adults. However, it is not necessary to have insight into your parents' psyche in order to do something more important: get insight into how becoming involved in their fight affected *you*. How were you affected by being the third, and least powerful, part of a three-person triangle where the two major players were at war? Did you feel engulfed by their war?

For each instance you list, write two or three sentences about how you felt as a child during these times. Then write two or three more sentences about each of these incidents, describing how you feel today about these instances.

Have you been involved in other situations that remind you of these early experiences of triangulation? If you experienced fear of being smothered in these later situations, how might this be related to your earlier experiences of being pulled into parental or adult conflict?

If you were (or are being) triangulated as an adult, describe two or three of these instances and then write three or four sentences about how being in this relatively powerless position is affecting you emotionally, physically, financially, and otherwise. Does the conflict, which isn't about you but involves you, feel smothering? If so, how?

11. Take a few minutes to slow down and reflect on the feelings you had wnhile completing this self-assessment. Did you feel numb, angry, amazed, confused, or afraid? Write two or three sentences about your reactions.

Donna had been triangulated by both her parents. Reflecting on her feelings as she completed this self-assessment, she noted that she had been objective and relatively emotion free. "I didn't feel numb, just totally rational and objective, as if I was thinking about a television program I had seen," she wrote in her journal.

But Donna *was* numb in that she was intellectualizing her feelings, rather than feeling them. Weeks after completing this exercise, Donna began to experience bouts of terror on Saturdays and Sundays despite the lack of any current dangers. She had a terrible feeling in her stomach, which she called despair, and she felt like she wasn't really alive—that she was a nonperson. She desperately wanted to connect with someone, but she was afraid to call or be with anyone lest they suffocate her and she disappear altogether.

She didn't isolate entirely. She would see her boyfriend, but she found herself fearing he would engulf her and began making sarcastic remarks to push him away. Her guilt over hurting her boy-friend, who had done nothing to harm her, drove her to her journal where she wrote:

> I'm so scared . . . pure terror. I don't know what to do next. This is exactly how I felt as a child, when both parents were pulling at me. My dad wanted me to be his; my mom wanted me to be hers. I was so afraid if I didn't fill their needs, they would fight and get a divorce and it would be all my fault. Here I was, seven years old—and afterward—trying to figure out what to do. I didn't know what to do, but I knew I was supposed to do something to stop them from fighting.
>
> I'd go to my mom and I'd feel so suffocated when she told me all kinds of bad things about my dad, cried about how mean he was, and ask me to comfort her. Then my dad would itemize all the ways my mom failed him as a wife. My parents' feelings filled my psyche—especially on weekends, because that's when all three of us were home together. I never realized it until now, but as a kid I felt so alone and sad on weekends because I couldn't really help my parents. There was no one to take care of me and I didn't know how to take care of myself. I felt like an orphan, even though I wasn't. Maybe that's why to this day I feel frightened of weekends, and why even though I'm lonely, I'm afraid to be with people because I'm afraid they'll smother me emotionally, the way my parents did when I was a kid.

It's important to be aware of the feelings you have while you complete the exercises in this book and aware of the kinds of reactions these exercises might stimulate days afterward. Your reactions may hold important clues and information about parts of your past that are still influencing you today. You need as much awareness of your past as possible in order to cope with ghosts from the past and live more fully in the present.

Family Hardships

If one of your parents or caretakers had a history of trauma or severe stress and that parent, or the other parent, turned to you for emotional support, then your fear of engulfment as an adult may stem from being overwhelmed by the emotional pain, depression, rage, loneliness, or anxiety of your stressed parent—or your nonstressed parent, whose needs may not have been met by the parent suffering hardships.

In homes where one of the parents is overwrought or dysfunctional due to the strains imposed upon by the other parent's stress or trauma-related symptoms, it is not uncommon for one of the children to become a little adult or take emotional care of the mother or father. The childhoods of kids put in these caretakers roles can be almost totally engulfed by the effects of the stress or trauma on their parents. As these children mature, they may come to fear that all relationships will be as demanding and frustrating as their relationship with their parents. Because as children they learned that loving involves the emotional pain of seeing the loved one in pain and being relatively powerless to help, and because that emotional pain was overwhelming, they may avoid intimate relationships or have problems in intimate relationships.

Emotional claustrophobia can arise among children of parents who have been traumatized when those children become traumatized by the parent's trauma. This process, called "secondary traumatization," has been found not only among children of combat veterans with post-traumatic stress disorder (PTSD), but among children of the survivors of the Nazi-perpetrated Holocaust (Matsakis 1996; Rosenheck 1985, 1986). In secondary traumatization, the child, in some manner, relives the parent's or other close relative's trauma or becomes obsessed with the trauma-related issues that trouble and concern the relative. The child may even manifest symptoms similar to those of the stressed relative, possibly having nightmares about the trauma or worring a great deal about death and injury.

I have observed several children and young adults evidencing secondary traumatization. Some displayed symptoms of post-traumatic stress disorder, such as an obsession with power and violence, difficulties concentrating, irritability, and rage reactions. Some children who suffer from secondary traumatization may assume a "rescuer" role in relation to the traumatized family member. In other cases, the rescuer role may be assumed by another child in the family who takes it upon himself or herself to make the traumatized relative happy (Rosenheck 1985, 1986). These children often spend an inordinate amount of time with the traumatized family member and may make that family member their best, if not only, friend.

Children who were engulfed by parental trauma may experience fear of engulfment in future close relationships, whether personal or occupational, or with respect to goal-oriented projects. For example, Andrea adopted a caretaker and rescuer role toward her father. When her combat veteran father had flashbacks and anxiety attacks, it was Andrea who moved furniture and objects out of his way. While her mother and sisters hid in their bedrooms, Andrea brought her father back to reality by softly comforting him and reminding him that he was safe at home, not at war.

But when she became sixteen, Andrea rebelled against her role as "helper girl." Crying out that she wanted to be herself, not a nursemaid, she defied parental authority and societal norms by taking up drugs and alcohol. She had spent so much of her life in the shadow of her father's pain and her mother's desperation that she wanted someone to finally pay attention to her and take care of her emotional needs. Yet whenever any of her friends or associates, male or female, began to show some emotional need or to share some of their sorrows, Andrea began arguments or found ways to end the relationship. She fled from others for fear she would be suffocated by the other person's pain the same way she had been engulfed by that of her parents.

Self-Assessment for the Effects of Family Trauma

On a fresh piece of paper in your journal entitled "Effects of Family Trauma," answer the following questions to the best of your ability:

1. Was anyone in your family subject to severe stress or trauma, such as war, rape, criminal assault, a vehicular or mechanical accident, or other type of life-threatening experience?

2. Were you (or are you) in any way preoccupied with that person's trauma or emotional state?

3. Did you try to assist the traumatized or stressed family member? Do you feel that helping this individual was ever the primary or main goal of your life?

4. If you didn't try to help the traumatized person, were you involved in helping someone else in the family who was overburdened as the result of the traumatized person's limitations or emotional problems? Do you feel that supporting this person was ever a dominant focus of your life?

5. Do you (or did you) ever feel suffocated by the traumatized person's emotions or problems or by your efforts to help that person or others in the family? If so, what particular aspect of the situation did you find suffocating?

6. What were the positive aspects of having been involved in your family's drama? What strengths or benefits did you derive from your exposure to this aspect of life?

7. What were some of the negative effects of having been so close to a family member's pain? What aspects of your life were overshadowed by the enormity of that person's problems? What parts of you never developed as a result of that person's trauma?

8. Do you feel that some portion of your fear of engulfment that resulted from your involvement with a traumatized or overly burdened family member has been transferred into your present life? If so, how? More specifically, to what extent does a history of being burdened with a family struggling with severe stress or trauma affect your personal relationships? Your work relationships? Your ability to set limits on how much time and energy you will commit to certain volunteer or work projects? Does it dominate your current life, or does it have a certain specific impact? Explain.

9. What types of feelings did you experience while answering these questions? Did you experience anxiety, anger, fear of engulfment, or any other strong emotion?

Chapter 2

Did People or Events Outside Your Family Contribute?

Were You Ever Victimized or Traumatized?

If you have ever been financially or emotionally exploited, you've been victimized. You can consider yourself traumatized if your life or the lives of others were ever at risk as the result of a natural catastrophe, (i.e., earthquake, hurricane, or tornado) or as the result of a man-made catastrophe (i.e., a war, a vehicular accident, a technological disaster, a medical error, or a criminal attack). During any type of victimization or traumatic experience, we are engulfed by a negative force or power. Even if we emerge physically unharmed, it doesn't alter the fact that during these experiences, we were surrounded by the potential for bodily harm or death, and there was no perceived escape.

To be traumatized means to be held captive in a horrible situation where there is no escape or breathing room or where all possible avenues of escape involve danger or betrayal of some moral value. Being victimized or traumatized can lead to subsequent emotional claustrophobia, especially when confronted with people, places, or situations that remind you of the past. Furthermore, your fear of being smothered is infused with an additional fear—that of being harmed, killed, or mistreated, or of witnessing others being injured, killed, or misused.

Self-Assessment: Victimization/Traumatization

If you were abused in a family situation, return to chapter 1 and complete the "Self-Assessment: Physical and Sexual Abuse," and "Self-Assessment: Emotional Abuse." If you were victimized by someone or something outside of your family, answer the following questions on a fresh piece of paper in your journal entitled "Victimization/Traumatic Experiences." Try to write five or six sentences in reply to each.

1. How did it feel to be overpowered by forces stronger than yourself? Was emotional claustrophobia one of these feelings?

2. In what ways were you trapped or held captive?

3. At this very moment, how are you feeling? What are your reactions to answering these questions about being victimized in your past? (Refer to the "Cautions" section in the introduction for guidelines on monitoring your reactions.)

4. When you are in situations today in which you feel entrapped, do you experience any of the feelings you listed in question 1?

5. Does the emotional claustrophobia you experienced during your victimizing or a traumatizing experience affect the way you react to certain situations today? If so, how?

If you are currently being abused, consult the sections on physical and sexual abuse in chapter 1 and in appendix A and seek help immediately.

Do You Have Difficulties Setting Boundaries?

A boundary is a dividing line. In geography, a boundary defines the difference between one country and another. In nature, a boundary refers to the point where one type of substance begins and another ends, for example, where a river ends and land begins. Boundaries are used to define different species of animals, different age groups, different types of jobs and degrees. Without boundaries, there would be chaos. For example, without dividing lines on highways, speed limits, and other types of regulations, driving would become impossible.

Lack of boundaries also causes chaos in relationships. If you are unable to decide what you will or will not do or which people and activities you will permit in your life and in what capacity, life can feel unmanageable. Certain demands made upon you by your parents, friends, employers, and others are legitimate. However, other demands may extend beyond the bounds of your agreement or contract or beyond the reasonable needs of the relationship.

If you cannot refuse or modify the nonessential demands and expectations of others, they can easily overwhelm you. Your life may feel consumed by others. Your sense of self, your personal goals for your life, and the limits you have because of your emotional, physical, and spiritual needs may all be engulfed by what others demand of you. If you continually yield to the requests of others, you may ultimately betray who you really are and what you have to offer the world.

Is your emotional claustrophobia the result of difficulty setting boundaries in your relationships with others? Difficulty setting boundaries could easily be a problem for you if your parents were traumatized, if you were traumatized yourself, or if you experienced symbiotic or engulfing relationships in your past. However, you don't need to have had a traumatic history in order to have problems setting boundaries. You may have difficulties setting boundaries simply because you had poor role models for boundary setting or because your self-esteem is so low (at least in some situations) that you don't feel you have the right to have boundaries.

In your life, either as a child, adolescent, or adult, have you found yourself in situations where establishing boundaries (i.e., clearly stating your goals and needs; taking care of your emotional, physical, or spiritual needs; or pursuing your dreams) meant you were met with hostility and rejection? If so, you were faced with a terrible dilemma: Suffer the scorn, condemnation, or rejection of a person whom you cared about, or betray and violate yourself. Many people who encounter such resistance when they first begin to set boundaries as children or as adolescents learn to surrender their right to establish personal boundaries. Then, as adults, they may repeat the pattern of not setting limits on themselves or others, making their life feel suffocated by the expectations and demands of others.

Under ideal circumstances young children develop the ability to "(1) be emotionally attached to others yet maintain a separate sense of self, (2) say appropriate 'no's' to others without fear of loss of love, and (3) receive 'no's' from others without withdrawing emotionally" (Black and Enns 1999, 26). However, for many children, saying "no" to non-essential demands made by parents and other family members is met with hostility and rejection. As a result, children can learn to feel guilty and afraid when setting personal boundaries, feelings that can persist into adolescence and adulthood.

Boundaries and Women

Traditionally society has given men more permission to set boundaries than women. Women have been expected to be comforters, soothers, and nurturers who are always available to serve the needs of others. Women have historically been held responsible for the emotional well-being of their family members and have been expected to create harmony in relationships, both at home and at work, even if it means giving more than they want to give or more than they can give without compromising their own needs and desires.

The woman's movement and the many social and cultural changes that have occurred in recent decades have made it increasingly acceptable for women to set boundaries in their relationships. However, old expectations die hard and many women still get the message that they should accommodate themselves to the needs of others, especially men and children.

Women who try to set boundaries for themselves must grapple not only with external resistance to their boundary setting, but with internal resistance. It is not only others who may feel (or tell) a woman that she is being unfeminine, "bitchy," or "aggressive," if she tries to set boundaries—the woman herself may be similarly self-critical because she is breaking the expectations she has been taught to have of herself.

On the other hand, women can also be hard on themselves for having insufficient boundaries or for not persisting in enforcing their boundaries when they meet opposition from others, especially family members. "If I say 'no' to something that violates my boundaries, my mother-in-law, who never worked a day in her life outside the home, calls me a selfish women's libber," explains June. "I'm furious because she just doesn't understand the pressures of being a working mother. But a part of me agrees with her. Just like her, I was raised to think I was an 'earth mother' who could be all things to all people and take care of half the universe without blinking an eye. Yet, if I change my mind and go along with what she or someone else wants, I beat myself up for abandoning my feminist principles and feel as if I have gotten an F in feminism."

A woman can feel engulfed when she feels torn between two principles, lifestyles, or commitments, each of which she deeply cherishes and which she believes are valid and worthy in their own right. Like June, many women today find value in the traditional nurturing, relational, and expressive roles that have historically been reserved for women. However, they may also wish to move beyond the limitations of these roles and embrace qualities and activities which have traditionally been reserved for men only. A woman's unique way of combining the old and the new is her individual right. She can select which of the old values she wishes to keep and which she wishes to discard or modify to meet her needs. She also has the right to choose from the new options open to her and not feel pressured to embrace all of them unquestioningly, just as she may have been forced to accept all of the old roles without question.

Women, like men, have the right to set the boundaries they need for their own mental health, regardless of whether or not those boundaries meet the approval of significant others or match popular trends. Furthermore, a woman's choices may vary and evolve over time, just as other parts of her being change and evolve as she changes or the demands made upon her change.

This creation of a new individualized role, which combines aspects of both the traditional roles and the modern roles for women, requires setting considerable boundaries. Such boundary setting is not easy and can lead to emotional claustrophobia when the choices are between aspects of being that are each fundamental and extremely important to her. The emotional claustrophobia can be even more intense when a woman needs to set boundaries on what she will and will not do for others, since she is likely to meet opposition from others. She may also find opposition from within herself, since a large part of a woman's self-esteem is often bound up with her relational roles as partner, mother, or daughter, and with her other relationships.

For example, a mother who is struggling to set boundaries on her work or her parenting responsibilities in order to be a working mother can easily feel engulfed because many of the expectations and obligations of these roles are legitimate and necessary. She may not easily be able tailor her work life or her mothering to accommodate both roles at a level with which she feels comfortable, because the responsibilities involved in both of these roles can be enormous. Especially at first, it may well feel overwhelming and impossible to successfully combine these roles. She may feel engulfed by the task, as well as psychologically trapped by the fact that she cannot simply ignore her maternal feelings or, alternatively, her work life. Her devotion to her children (or partnership) may be as strong and as central to her self-esteem as her need to be productive and creative in the workforce outside the home.

In some instances, even the most creative and imaginative approaches to combining the two roles may be insufficient to meet the demands of the roles, or the woman's perception of what she feels she needs to do in order to be a success. This process of letting go of expectations for personal performance in each of these roles can be not only overwhelming, but extremely painful, and it can provoke fear of engulfment when a woman feels that she is betraying one important aspect of herself, for example, her work, in order to be loyal to another important part of herself, for example, her children. She may also feel engulfed and trapped when she realizes that she needs to lessen her expectations of herself in each of these roles in order to accommodate both, especially when the expectations she has for herself in each role may be important sources of her self-esteem.

What is engulfing is the recognition that, contrary to media messages, no one can "have it all." Difficult choices need to be made, but until they are made, the woman can be subject to bouts of emotional claustrophobia. She may feel flooded with fear, doubt, anxiety, and confusion as she tries to decide how to manage and juggle her numerous responsibilities and interests, as well as the performance expectations associated with each of these, with the realities of time limitations, schedule conflicts, energy limitations, and other obstacles.

Self-Assessment: Boundary Violations

Title a fresh piece of paper "Boundary Violations" and answer the following questions to the best of your ability:

1. Any type of emotional, physical, or sexual abuse constitutes a boundary violation. If you were emotionally, physically, or sexually abused, write four or five sentences about how somebody else's actions or words violated you.

2. How did others react when you refused a request that was not in your best interest or that was not part of your desires for your life? Was your refusal accepted, or were you told you were selfish, mean, short-sighted, irresponsible, or arrogant?

3. List three instances where your intentional choices were met with anger, name-calling, suspicion, rejection, or threats of rejection.

4. List three instances where your boundaries were accepted.

5. In general, have you been encouraged or discouraged from establishing boundaries?

6. Have you ever experienced emotional claustrophobia as the direct result of difficulty establishing or maintaining your boundaries?

For example, Jose learned that if he did not agree to every request made by his supervisor, even when it was not part of his job description or it violated company policy, he would be passed over for promotions and certain benefits. As a result, he said "yes" to everything asked of him, establishing no boundary between what he would or would not do. In doing so, he hoped to escape his supervisor's wrath.

But he also began to feel overextended and mistreated. The subsequent resentment and stress contributed to the development of various health problems, and his self-esteem suffered as well. Over time, he bagan to feel suffocated every time his supervisor approached him, even with a legitimate request.

If these types of experiences sound familiar, see appendix A for helpful books on improving personal boundaries.

All-or-Nothing Organizations and Belief Systems

Just as it is especially hard to set boundaries when confronted with an exceptionally strong personality, it is especially hard to set boundaries if you are or were part of a religious, political, social, or other type of organization that had all-or-nothing thinking. The rules for conduct and belonging are strict. Minor violations can mean various forms of harsh punishment, including exclusion from the group.

Also, much is expected. You are expected to give your all to the group, not small measured amounts. If you've belonged to a group that demanded strict allegiance and extreme loyalty and that made adhering to its rules and requirements a moral issue, then you might be particularly vulnerable to feeling suffocated.

If you are currently a member of such a group and are experiencing difficulties with the group because you feel they are expecting too much of you, you may experience emotional claustrophobia in your relationships with members of the group. This emotional claustrophobia, based on your experience with the group, may transfer to persons outside the group when they make demands on you or expect your loyalty.

Self-Assessment: All-or-Nothing Organizations or Belief Systems

On a fresh page in your journal entitled "All-or-Nothing Thinking," answer the following questions to the best of your ability:

1. Were you or are you currently a member of an organization or group that demands strict loyalty and rigid adherence to a certain set of rules and principles? Examples of such groups include the military, the police force, and other occupations where conformity is required due to the nearly constant life-threat involved, as well as certain religious and social groups.

2. Did you ever feel that adhering to these expectations consumed your life or personality? Write five or six sentences about what is or was expected of you in this organization and the ways in which it dominated your interests, relationships, and self-concept.

3. As a result of these experiences, do you have difficulty seeing moderate or partial solutions to problems? Do you instead tend to view matters in extreme terms, as totally right or totally wrong or as completely necessary or completely frivolous? Write three or four sentences about how this experience has affected your ability to view situations as being complex and unclear.

4. Today, in the present, are you able to commit yourself partially to an organization or person, or do you feel you have to commit yourself totally or not at all? When you do commit yourself, do you ever experience emotional claustrophobia?

5. Do you avoid even partial commitments to persons or organizations in order to avoid the emotional claustrophobia you feel when making any type of commitment?

If you have answered yes to any of these questions, write five or six sentences about how your experience has affected your ability to become involved with people and organizations in the present.

Difficult Human Emotions

All emotions have a physical aspect, especially anger, sexual excitement, and fear. These three emotions involve noticeable physiological arousal or heightened response of the autonomic nervous system. When the autonomic nervous system is aroused, the pupils of the eyes tend to dilate; the skin tends to perspire; the heart rate accelerates; digestion is inhibited (sometimes leading to nausea and other stomach discomforts) and the adrenal glands secrete stress hormones to prepare the body for action. In these respects, anger, fear, and sexual arousal have much in common.

These three emotions feel very different. Yet when these three emotions are intensely stimulated, they have something in common: the people experiencing them feel as if they might lose control of their bodies—a potentially frightening state of being. Consequently, you may experience emotional claustrophobia when certain relationships bring to the fore one of these emotions, which can literally flood your body and cause drastic alterations in your heart rate, hormone production, breathing, and temperature.

To be an emotionally alive person is a challenging proposition. On the one hand, you will experience the joys of being attuned to love, tenderness, wonder, and joy. On the other hand, even those of you who have been in therapy or self-help programs for many years may need to struggle with emotions that can create conflict, confusion, and stress. These emotions include anger, sexual excitement, and fear.

Little children often dream of dragons and monsters who are trying to catch and harm them. One interpretation of such dreams is that children are dreaming about the monster or demon within themselves, for example, their anger or their sexual feelings. The monster in the dream could also represent fear of the unknown and personal insecurities about maturing. As children are increasingly expected to face life on their own without their parents, their growing independence can be a source of pride, but it can also be a scary proposition.

Just as children have nightmares about being devoured by monsters that represent their own difficult feelings, your fear of engulfment may stem from some of the difficulties you have managing the all-too-human feelings of anger, sexual arousal, or anxiety. If a certain individual or situation causes you to react with a degree of rage, physical desire, or anxiety that you feel you can't manage or that you find unacceptable, you may experience your reaction as fear of being smothered. In such circumstances, the fear of being suffocated is an expression of other fears, such as fears of specific emotions or fear of the intensity of certain emotions.

Self-Assessment: Difficult Human Emotions

Set aside three fresh pages in your journal. Entitle one page "Anger," the next, "Anxiety," and the third, "Sexual Arousal." For the purposes of this exercise, use the following definitions of anger, anxiety, and arousal:

- Anger, in general, is a fairly strong emotional reaction that accompanies numerous situations, such as being psychologically or physically restrained or interfered with, having one's possessions taken or removed, being attacked or threatened, or being insulted or ignored. Anger usually involves a strong physical reaction, including increased heart rate, feelings of agitation and restlessness, and surges of adrenaline.

- Anxiety is a vague, unpleasant emotional state characterized by apprehension, dread, distress, and uneasiness regarding a future (not a past) event. Anxiety is a future-oriented emotion, something you experience when you expect a negative or undesirable occurrence.

- Arousal refers to feeling excited on the hormonal, glandular, or muscular level.

With these definitions in mind, try to answer the following questions for each emotion:

1. As a child or adolescent, what were you told about anger (or anxiety or sexual arousal)? Were you told that having any of these feelings was a sign of moral depravity, moral weakness, or some other negative personality trait? Were you given mixed messages about any of these fundamental human states? Refer to your self-assessment entitled "Were You Expected to Do or Be the Impossible?" in chapter 1, where you identified the "shoulds" you were exposed to as a child. Do any of these concern anger (or anxiety or sexual arousal)?

2. How comfortable are you with your anger (or your sexuality or your levels of anxiety)?

3. Do you feel you are able to handle these feelings when they are intense, or do you fear these emotions because of their potential to overwhelm you and make you feel out of control?

4. Have you ever lost control of yourself or regretted your behavior when you have become extremely angry (or anxious or lustful)?

5. Write five or six sentences about how you react when overcome with anger (or anxiety or physical desire). As you feel anger (or anxiety or desire) rising within you, do you become afraid of yourself? Do you then feel engulfed by your own emotions?

Grief

Another difficult human emotion is grief. Grieving and coping with losses are among the most difficult aspects of human existence. Emotionally, grieving is such a challenge that most people, both those with emotional claustrophobia and others, tend to avoid it at all costs.

How much easier it is to be angry than sad! When you are angry, you surge with adrenaline and rage. You know you are alive. Even when you are anxious, you feel alive. But when you are grieving, it can feel like you're a collapsed balloon. The pain of loss engulfs you and you feel vulnerable, defenseless, and weak. And you hurt. You may hurt so much that you feel like you are dying inside.

People who are actively grieving often feel as if their grief has engulfed their entire life, suffocating all other interests and concerns. But people who have repressed their grief or who are fighting their grief can be even more emotionally claustrophobic. People who are actively grieving may be smothered by their sadness, but by feeling it they are slowly delivering themselves from it. If they grieve sufficiently, they will pass through the intense period of grieving where grieving engulfs one's emotions and life.

But people who have yet to grieve or who have grieved incompletely may often feel smothered when a certain situation or person touches on their grief, thus awakening the awareness of the loss and the sad feelings that go with this awareness. When this awareness is shoved away—because a person is afraid to grieve, is not permitted to grieve by others, or does not have the time or place to grieve—the unexpressed grief can suffocate the person's psyche and be experienced as a form of emotional claustrophobia.

One common difficulty is not recognizing all of your losses. While everyone understands losses, such as a death in the family, the loss of a limb, or the loss of a love relationship, there are other losses that merit mourning; for example, the loss of an opportunity for self-actualization, the loss of innocence, or the loss of hope that a particular wish will come true.

For example, Dorothy was able to trace her emotional claustrophobia during the holidays to the fact that she never had children. For years she had pretended that it didn't matter that she and her husband had been unable to have children. She had a husband who adored her and a satisfying career. But during one holiday season when visiting her family and seeing her siblings with their many children, Dorothy realized that the reason she experienced emotional claustrophobia during the holidays was her deep sadness that she could never bear children. Once she was able to grieve this loss, her feelings of suffocation surrounding holiday dinners greatly diminished.

Self-Assessment: Grief

1. What emotional, financial, vocational, social, or personal losses have you experienced in your life? Can you identify at least five?

2. For each loss, do you feel that you acknowledged this loss sufficiently? Do you feel you fully grieved this loss?

3. Do you see any relationship between any of these losses and feeling smothered when something or someone reminds you of this loss?

Engulfing Personalities

Sometimes your emotional claustrophobia has little to do with you. People who are aggressive, menacing, overbearing, intrusive, demanding, or extremely authoritarian evoke fear of engulfment in many of us. Overbearing, aggressive people may actually desire to use your time and energy for their purposes and may not hesitate to utilize their physical or emotional power to coerce you into going along with their desires. Similarly, people who are emotionally or financially needy (or who are severely ill) may try to make you feel guilty for being more fortunate than they are in order to persuade you to give more of your time, money, or self than you wish. Because their needs are so many and so intense, you may literally feel that interacting with them would mean the end of you.

On the other hand, people who are extremely charming, sexually attractive, or charismatic can also create fears of being smothered. Their very attractiveness may feel overwhelming and you may feel you could be smothered if you spend time with them. Whether exceptionally attractive and powerful or exceptionally devious or cruel, intense personalities can present a challenge even to those who are adept and experienced at setting boundaries in their relationships. If, however, your are still learning how to set boundaries, encountering such people can easily trigger emotional claustrophobia.

Most difficult to handle are personalities who are overpowering in both negative and positive ways, such as Sylvia's supervisor, Freda. Sylvia had worked hard in therapy to learn to say no to the many requests made of her by her widowed mother. She was also able to set boundaries on the sexual advances of others. Sylvia received numerous awards for her excellent performance on the job and enjoyed her work so much that she was willing to work extra hours for free. Her relationships with her superiors and coworkers were relatively problem free, until, for no apparent reason, her supervisor, Freda, began to give her poor ratings and issued orders that hindered Sylvia's ability to complete her projects.

Freda ordered that all the furniture be removed from Sylvia's office, ostensibly because new furniture was ordered. But for months the new furniture never came and Sylvia had to move from one office to another, depending on which office might be available because another worker was not in the office. Once she even had to work in the hallway.

Freda was extremely bright, articulate, and exceptionally talented in her profession. She had helped to train Sylvia and had complimented Sylvia on her abilities. But now at staff meetings, Freda made derogatory comments about Sylvia's work performance and hinted that Sylvia had a "personality problem." When Sylvia voiced her concerns, her speaking up was perceived by Freda as evidence that Sylvia had an "argumentative, antisocial" personality and that she was "disrupting" the office environment.

But Freda wasn't always degrading Sylvia or making her life difficult. Sometimes she dazzled Sylvia with her expertise and treated Sylvia as she had in the past: with courtesy and respect. Nevertheless, whenever Freda came near her or telephoned her, Sylvia felt suffocated and smothered. Sometimes her emotional claustrophobia was so intense, she made errors in her work or stuttered when she spoke, which made her even more anxious, which caused her to make even more errors, all of which were observed and commented on by Freda.

"Every time Freda even walks down the hall, I feel engulfed—and paralyzed," Sylvia explains. "Sometimes Freda doesn't even talk to or look at me and when she does speak to me, she isn't always nasty. But other times she is. Am I crazy to react this way? I'm afraid I'm going to lose my job—not because of her—but because I feel so suffocated I'm going to keep messing up."

Another problem was that Sylvia's fear of engulfment had spread to any situation involving work projects. She began to feel smothered when coworkers or part-time help (who were used to taking direction from her) approached her. Eventually, just being in the office made her feel suffocated and stifled. She decided to look for another job, yet she feared that she could not present herself well to potential employers due to the emotional claustrophobia that she was now coming to experience in almost all offices and work-related discussions, especially with persons whose skills she admired.

Self-Assessment: Engulfing Personalities

On a fresh piece of paper in your journal entitled "Engulfing Personalities," answer the following questions to the best of your abilities:

1. Review the last five or six years of your life. Have you met or worked with any individuals with overpowering personalities, either due to their positive traits, their negative traits, or their emotional or financial need? For each person, write two sentences about what aspect of their personalities felt overwhelming to you.

If you'd like to go back further in your life and note the names of persons whose personal powers resulted in your fear of engulfment, you may do so now or at a later time. But it is important not to overwhelm yourself in answering these questions. Let your reactions be your guide and consult the "Cautions" section in the introduction for guidelines on assessing and managing your reactions to answering these questions.

2. In each of the three cases you selected in question 1, think back on your interaction and answer the following questions: How did you react to these people? Was fear of engulfment one of the ways you responded? Did you also have other fears or reactions? If so, what were they?

Note that it is perfectly possible to have both negative and positive reactions to strong individuals. For example, you can admire a person's dedication to a charitable cause, yet resent the pressure that person puts on you for more of your time and money. You can despise a supervisor's dictatorial manner, yet admire her professional skills.

3. Do you feel your emotional claustrophobia is primarily a direct response to a specific trait (or traits) in the other individual? If so, which trait? If that person was only half as intelligent, attractive, poor, politically powerful, deceitful, manipulative, or whatever strong quality they possess, do you think you would fear being suffocated by them?

Chapter 3

How Has Emotional Claustrophobia Impacted Your Life?

Those of you have been in twelve-step programs such as AA, NA, OA, or Al-Anon may be familiar with the fourth step, taking a "fearless and searching" moral inventory of yourself. Usually this step consists of making list of persons who you think you have hurt, either intentionally or unintentionally, during your days of drinking, drugging, overeating, or starving yourself, as the result of the fears and anxieties which underlay the substance abuse.

One of the persons who should definitely be on this list of injured parties is yourself. After completing the fourth step you may see how you let yourself down, injured yourself, or allowed others to take advantage of you or how certain fears controlled your life.

In this chapter, you are going to take an inventory of your fear of engulfment, taking a close look at the specific characteristics of the emotional claustrophobia in your life and how it has impacted on your self-esteem, your relationships, and your life goals.

This task may seem overwhelming, but you will only be asked to focus on a few select experiences of this fear, and you will be guided in completing this task one step at a time.

The Importance of a Personal Inventory

Until you know the specific nature of your fear, you cannot begin to address it. Having a mental picture or "map" of your emotional claustrophobia can help you better assess how this fear is affecting your life and how you can start to control the negative effects of this fear on your self-esteem, relationships, or life goals. You cannot begin to make changes in your life until you become aware of your existing habits and behaviors. Furthermore, clinical research indicates that the process of recording fears and anxieties can be a valuable aid in managing these fears (Zuercher-White 1998). Simply taking the time to write about your life indicates that you feel that your life, and your time, are important.

As you continue reading this book, you will be better able to answer the following questions. As you answer these questions in your notebook, leave plenty of space after each response in case you decide to come back and review your writing later and add to it.

Beginning Your Inventory

Fear of the Inventory

Are you afraid to start your inventory? Do you fear that as you reply to these questions, you might experience that horrible fear all over again or that the fear might even increase? What are you afraid you might feel? Are you afraid of experiencing emotional pain, confusion, inner emptiness, or some other feeling? What are you afraid you might do? What specifically do you fear you might do or say? Are you afraid you might lose control in some manner? Write five or six sentences about these fears.

While writing about your emotional claustrophobia can bring to the fore some unpleasant memories, the understanding you will gain about your emotional claustrophobia is the first step toward mastering it. However, if you feel that the agony of these feelings will overwhelm you or that you will not be able to control your behavior, or if your fear of engulfment is rooted in traumatic incidents for which you have not received adequate help, you may need to stop reading this book and seek professioanl help before you come back to it. Review the suggestions made in the "Cautions" section in the introduction of this book to see if you should consult with a mental health professional before you proceed.

If you feel comfortable continuing, answer the following questions as thoroughly and honestly as you can. Remember to leave plenty of space between your replies so you can return and write more later.

Your Goals

1. Why did you buy this book? Were you prompted to buy this book by a recent incident? If so, write five or six sentences about this incident and why it propelled you to take action regarding your fear of engulfment.

2. What do you hope this book will help you accomplish? Can you list three or four goals that you hope this book will help you achieve?

3. After you purchased this book, how did you feel about having bought it? Were you optimistic about finding some help for yourself or did you wonder if you were about to waste your time, just like you had wasted your money?

If one part of you felt hopeless, but another part felt hopeful enough to purchase the book anyway, this suggests that your sense of hope is greater than your sense of hopelessness. As you read on in this book, you will find more and more ways to overcome your fears and exert more control over your life, which should greatly increase your sense of hope for the future.

Does any part of you feel ashamed for purchasing this book? Why is that the case? Would you feel ashamed at having any type of fear or is there something particularly shameful about the fear of engulfment, as opposed to other fears? Write a few sentences about your feelings of shame: How strong are they? Can you trace the origins of your feelings of shame to a parent, relative, neighbor, or teacher? To a religious, military, or political leader? Or to some other important person in your life who told you that emotional claustrophobia was a sign of weakness or moral deficiency? If you are male, were you ever told that being afraid wasn't masculine?

If you did experience considerable shame or fear about having this book, then your wish to understand and cope with your fear of being smothered must be exceptionally strong, so strong that you overcame your reluctance to deal with the subject. This is an indication that somewhere within you exists a strong desire to grow and master this fear. Give yourself credit for trying to change, despite any negative emotions you may have regarding such change.

Fear of Engulfment Inventory

Brainstorming

Entitle a page in your journal "Brainstroming." On this page, make a list of the situations and people who elicit your fear of engulfment. Do not edit the list as you are writing it. Simply make the list, leaving room to add additional information or incidents later. Include the incidents you recorded in your journal for chapters 1 and 2.

Organizing

The various situations you have listed probably vary in the intensity and duration of the fear of engulfment. In this exercise, you will be asked to divide the incidents you listed into four categories:

1. Situations in which the fear is the easiest to endure.

2. Situations you feel you might be able to handle after a few months of therapy, recovery, or working on your fear of engulfment with this book.

3. Situations you might be able to confront in a few years (maybe).

4. Situations you plan to avoid for the rest of your life.

Entitle a new page in your journal "Organizing" and draw lines to make four columns. Label them from left to right, "Easiest to Handle," "Possibly Manageable Within a Year," "Possibly Manageable in the Distant Future," and "Impossible to Ever Handle."

Now take your list from your brainstorming exercise and place each fear-producing situation in the appropriate category.

Selecting Three Situations to Work On

When you feel ready to confront a situation involving fear of engulfment, select one situation from the column "Easiest to Handle." Beginning with a more difficult situation, such as one in column two or three, can be a setup for failure. No trigger situation, even one you classified as relatively easy to handle, is truly easy. You have to start somewhere, though, so it is best to start where you have the greatest chance of success. The incident you select should be a situation that you expect you'll have to confront again, not a situation that you feel will never reoccur. You will be more motivated to work hard on decreasing your fear of the fearful situation if you know there is a practical value for your efforts.

What Happened?

In this section, you will try to recreate the incident in the form of a narrative or story in as detailed a manner as possible. Answer the following questions to the best of your ability:

What happened first? What happened next? What happened after that, etc.? Who was with you? What did that person (or those people) say or do? What did you say or do? Describe the physical location. Was it indoors, outdoors, or in a particular type of room? When did it happen? Note the time of the day, the date, the month, and the season. Were there any unusual circumstances involved?

Review what you have written thus far. What do you think started the fear? Was it something another individual did or said, or was it something you did, thought, or felt? Were there any stated or unstated demands being made of you by the other person or by the situation? What were these demands or expectations? Did any of these initiate or contribute to your fear? Are you aware of any other origins of this fear, for example, prior frightening experiences in your life? Write at least three or four sentences in reply to each of these questions.

Did the fear develop slowly and gradually in stages or were you feeling relatively fine one moment and suddenly overcome with fear the next? Was there a particular aspect of the situation that caused you to cross the line between feeling mildly uncomfortable and becoming truly frightened? If so, at what point did you start feeling as if you were losing control?

Was this particular episode with fear of engulfment unique, or is it an experience you have often?

What Was the Fear Like?

What did your emotional claustrophobia feel like? List five adjectives that describe it. Now write three or four sentences about how the fear felt. While you were experiencing the fear, were there any changes in intensity or was the fear relatively constant?

Had you experienced fear of engulfment in this situation before or was it the first time? If it wasn't the first time, when did you experience it in the past? Under what circumstances? Were you experiencing any other feelings in addition to the fear (e.g. anger, anxiety sexual arousal, confusion)?

Your Physical Reactions

Fear is created not only by the actual danger involved, but also by your physical reactions to the fear and by the thoughts and beliefs you have about that fear and your ability to cope with it effectively. In this part of the inventory, you will try to identify the way your body reacts to fear of engulfment; in a later section, you will address the kinds of thoughts and beliefs that your fear of engulfment generates in your mind.

Our culture tends to view the mind and body as separate entities. However, whenever you feel something powerful, like fear or stress, your body reacts in certain predictable ways, such as body tension or even pain. The first step in dealing with this tension is to be aware of its existence. If you are like many people in our society, you may be more aware of your "to-do" list and the state of your bank account than of the tension in your own body. But knowing where you tend to feel the tension in your body when you experience fear of engulfment is critical in being able to manage the situation.

Thinking back to the situation you are examining in detail, try to recall the state of your body. Close your eyes for a few minutes and imagine you are back in that situation—engulfed by the fear of engulfment. Now scan your body. Start with your toes and move up your body asking yourself, "Where is the tension? Is it in my toes, feet, calves, knees, thighs, genitals, buttocks, abdominal area, chest, neck, jaw, forehead, ears, eyes, or some other part of the body?" Another approach is to ask yourself "What parts of my body come into awareness first? Which parts can I easily feel and which have little sensation? Do I feel any physical discomfort at all?"

Do not rush this exercise. As you become aware of the way your body responded while you experienced fear of engulfment, try to stay with the awareness for five or ten minutes. Observe if the tension or discomfort moves or changes.

Then answer the following questions in your notebook: How did you react physically? Did your body show signs of anxiety, such as nausea or butterflies in your stomach, hyperventilation, weakness all over, dizziness, tremors, rapid heartbeat, sweating, dry mouth, feelings of warmth, or shaking? Did you experience muscle tension, headaches, or pain in other parts of your body?

While some people become anxious and hyperalert when they're afraid, others experience a numbing response. Did you feel you "shut down," in that you felt physically lifeless and emotionally numb? Did you experience any difficulties with memory, speaking, or thinking, such as speeded up thoughts or confusion? Did you feel fatigued or dizzy, or find it difficult to move? Write about five or six sentences about the physical reactions you experienced. Be as specific as possible.

What Did the Fear Make You Do or Say?

What did you do or say after you were aware you were afraid?

Distancing is a way to handle strong or overwhelming emotions. Did you try to leave the situation physically? If so, how did you make your exit? Did you make a sarcastic remark, start a fight, or use a false excuse, such as illness or an unforseen work commitment? Did you distance yourself mentally, by "tuning out" or "spacing out"?

Did you try to cover up your reaction with humor? Did you try to get the focus off yourself onto something or someone else?

Did you try to cope with the fear by turning to a substance, such as alcohol, drugs, or excess food, or by going on a shopping spree? Did you try to distract yourself from the fear by watching television or videos? Did you try to distract yourself by acting seductive, masturbating, watching or reading pornography, or having sexual contact with someone you wouldn't have touched if you weren't under the influence of fear of engulfment?

Some of the typical ways people deal with fear of engulfment include emotional and physical distancing, or increased relationships with nonhumans (plants, animals, or inanimate objects). Some forms of spiritual searching can also be escapes from fear of engulfment in human relationships. However, for others, fear of engulfment prevents spiritual or religious pursuits.

What Were You Telling Yourself?

"As a man thinketh, so is he," is an oft-quoted Biblical saying (Proverbs 23:7). The truth in this statement is that the way you talk to yourself affects both the way you act and the way you feel. Psychologists call it self-talk or inner monologue, referring to how all of us are constantly "talking to ourselves" in our head.

In this exercise, you will try to recall what you were thinking during the incident. Trace your self-talk or inner monologue as best you can. Also try to remember what you were thinking shortly prior to the incident.

Pay special attention to any critics that live inside your head—voices that tell you that you are thinking, feeling, or doing something wrong or shameful. For example, how were you evaluating your physical or emotional reactions during the time you were experiencing fear of engulfment? If you broke out into a sweat, did you accept that as a normal reaction to anxiety and fear, or did you see yourself as a weakling or failure for having this reaction?

Did your inner critics ever place you in a "no-win" situation: that is, no matter what you did, felt, or thought, you were blameworthy or incompetent? For example, suppose you decided to leave the situation causing emotional claustrophobia rather than endure the pain of it. How did you view this decision to leave? Did you see it as a sign of cowardice that you did not have the fortitude to "stick it out to the end," or did you see it as a way of taking care of yourself? On the other hand, if you decided to "stick it out to the end," did you subsequently berate yourself for not having had the courage to get up and leave, or did you applaud yourself for having the courage to endure? Often how we view our decisions is more significant than the decisions themselves.

Your Beliefs

Your beliefs guide your thoughts, feelings, and actions. Yet if you are like many people, you may have trouble identifying the beliefs that govern you and putting them into words. In this section of the inventory, you will write down what you were believing during your engulfing experiences. If you can track the course of your beliefs before, during, and after these episodes of fear, you will be better able take control over your thinking processes when confronted again with fearful situations.

What were you believing just before, during, and after the period of time you experienced the fear of being smothered? Imagine yourself back in the situation where you experienced the fear. What were the specific thoughts you had about yourself, the other individual, or the situation?

Did your beliefs change during the course of the episode? Can you remember what your thoughts were just before the fear began? Don't ignore or minimize the early stages of your fear of engulfment. The thoughts you had during this period may have determined the increase in fear that followed.

What were you thinking or believing when your emotional claustrophobia was at its height? As it began to diminish? Did you feel trapped? Did you fear you would lose your mind, faint, have a heart attack, or die? Did you worry that others were observing and judging? Did you believe that you could not possibly survive the situation alone, despite there being no help available?

People who suffer from fear of engulfment typically believe they are trapped and have no choices—that is, that they are powerless. They also tend to believe that they are incompetent and they cannot control themselves, that they are defective or not as important as the other people involved (and therefore do not have the right to stand up for themselves or express their feelings or needs), that if they do express themselves, something terrible will happen, or that simply being afraid will kill them. "Once I start writing, I go into a panic. I feel I'm going to be sucked into a deep tunnel and die," explains Teresa, a freelance fiction writer. "It's hard to forge ahead doing what you think you were born to do artistically, yet feel you are being suffocated by it."

The belief that you are trapped, and powerless, and that you have no choices may sound like: "I'm stuck here. I can't leave. I guess I'll just have to suffer. I can't speak up. I can't defend myself. I've been a wimp all my life and I'm too old to change. I don't have a choice. I have to act as I have in the past or disaster will follow. I am going to die. I can't say no to this person. I can't let this person near me or they will destroy me. If I don't say anything, maybe things will change for the better. There's no point in rocking the boat. If I do what I usually do, nothing unexpected will go wrong."

The belief that you are incompetent and can't control yourself includes thoughts such as: "I won't be able to handle this and I'll just blow up or disappear. There must be something very wrong with me because I keep having emotional claustrophobia. I can't trust myself to focus on myself when I'm near this person. I won't be able to take care of myself with this person nearby. If I get near this person I'll feel so anxious I won't be able to think and I'll make lots of mistakes. I'm afraid that I will automatically refuse all of their requests just to insure that they don't smother me and say no even to their reasonable requests. I'm also afraid that I will become so afraid of automatically rejecting and distancing myself from this person that I will try to compensate for being so irrational by agreeing to everything they want and then be engulfed by them."

The belief that your needs and feelings are of lesser value than those of the other person involved includes thoughts such as: "I am not a good person. I am not trustworthy. I am responsible for this person's health and happiness. I am unworthy. I am worthy, but the other person is more worthy than I am. The other person's happiness is more important than mine. My needs are important, but the other person's needs are more important than my needs. I can take the abuse/disappointment because I am strong—they are weak. They couldn't take it if I drew a line or boundary. I belong to them (him/her). My purpose is to please them. If I don't, I've failed as a daughter (son, employer). My self-esteem depends on their approval. I'll feel ashamed and worthless if I don't do what they want or expect."

As you put your thoughts on paper, try to be as specific as possible. If you are having trouble putting your beliefs into words or being specific about your beliefs, consider four strategies that follow (Zuercher-White 1998):

1. Write down whatever comes to your mind. Don't try to edit your thoughts. Include rational as well as irrational thoughts.

2. Try to visualize yourself back in the situation where you felt the fear of engulfment. Imagine the physical setting, what you were wearing or carrying, the time of day, and other such details. Then ask yourself, "What was I thinking?" "Then, what did I think after that? And after that?"

3. If you remember feeling you were going to die or explode or fade away, ask yourself how exactly would you die, explode, or fade away?

4. If you draw a blank in identifying your thoughts or beliefs, then stop working on this exercise and involve yourself in a current situation that makes you feel somewhat afraid. For example, suppose you are afraid to ask your supervisor for a day off. As you walk toward the supervisor's office, observe what you are thinking and feeling. These thoughts and feelings may give you valuable clues to the thoughts you have during episodes of emotional claustrophobia.

Feeling Trapped

In what ways did you feel trapped in the situation? What trapped you? What opposing needs, beliefs, or pressures kept you stuck? While feeling terrified, did you promise yourself never to repeat this action, return to this physical location, or see this individual? While making this promise to yourself, were you aware that you probably would be unable to keep it? If so, why not? What circumstances, beliefs, or feelings would prevent you from avoiding this experience in the future?

Filling in the blanks in the following statements may help you identify competing attitudes, beliefs, and fears with which you were struggling:

1. I wanted to _____, but felt I could not because

_____ .

2. On the one hand, I felt I needed to _____ . On the other hand, I also needed to _____ .

3. I love/ am committed to / believe in /value _____ , but I also love/ am committed to / believe in /value _____

_____ .

4. I felt my most important priority at the time was _____ , but my other most important priority at the same time was

_____ .

Learning from Contradictions

After you selected an incident to work on, your first writing assignment was to try to recreate the incident in the form of a narrative or story in as detailed a manner as possible. Reread what you wrote in response to an earlier section of this chapter entitled "What Happened?" and ask yourself the following questions: How well did your emotional reactions to the events match with the events themselves?

For example, if you wrote about a happy time with a particular person, then noted that being with this person brought upon a terrible attack of fear of engulfment, how can you account for this discrepancy? Similarly, if you wrote about being abused by someone, then, in describing your feelings, did not indicate that you had any anger or negative feelings toward that person (only fear of engulfment) how can you explain the discrepancy?

If you can not make headway on this question, you may need to consult with a professional therapist. Your "stuckness" and the discrepancy between what happened and how you feel is an important issue in understanding the causes of your fear of engulfment.

Assessing the Costs

What price do you pay for having this fear of engulfment and for the way you react to it? In the particular situation you have chosen to focus on, describe the various ways you "pay" for having this fear or for the ways you respond to it. Ask yourself, what opportunities or experiences you are missing because of your struggle with the fear of engulfment? How is this fear limiting your involvement in life? Does it cause you to avoid everyday situations?

For example, is your family, social, or love life or your career development stymied by an inability to participate in certain types of activities due to fear of engulfment? What are the costs in time, money, or productivity in dealing with the aftereffects of going through an experience with this fear?

Some of the costs associated with fear of engulfment are listed below. Some may apply to you, others may not:

1. difficulty evaluating situations and people

2. difficulty concentrating

3. memory problems

4. difficulty seeing the whole picture, distortion of what is occurring

5. not motivated to learn new things or meet new people due to fear that doing something new or meeting someone new will disorganize you or make you feel numb

6. difficulty organizing your behavior to achieve a goal or to stay focused on a conversation or social interaction

7. impaired reasoning and other mental powers

8. more effort is involved in responding to situations and people that elicit fear of being smothered. It takes effort to calm down after experiencing this fear. When the effort seems too great, the tendency is to retreat from these people and situations because handling them demands a great deal of energy and effort

Be as specific as possible in answering this question of the price you pay for your emotional claustrophobia. Take a sheet of paper, label it "Costs" and divide it into five columns. Label the first column "Emotional Costs"; the second, "Financial Costs"; the third, "Health Costs"; the fourth, "Mental Costs"; and the fifth, "Other Costs."

For example, under the column "Emotional Costs" Amy wrote: "I'll never be able to build a serious romantic relationship unless I can overcome this emotional claustrophobia I feel if I'm on a date for over two hours. When I keep my dates short so I can manage them, I don't have the opportunity to truly get to know my date. Then I start feeling that because of my limitation, I'll never have the close committed relationship that I desire. To punish myself, I go on a food binge. The binging takes only an hour or two, but getting my physical energy and self-esteem back after a binge can take at least two days, during which I don't even think about going on a date. Sometimes I even stay home from work. That's what fear of engulfment costs me."

Under the column for financial costs, Amy wrote, "If I have to get up and take a walk every time I fear that the coworker next to me is about to eat me up, I won't get the job done and my supervisor will think I'm irresponsible. I'll start calling in sick rather than have to deal with the no-win choice of being afraid of being engulfed, or being afraid of being fired. But I can't call in sick forever and taking a lot of sick leave jeopardizes my job."

Under the column for medical costs, Amy listed asthma and bronchitis, two stress-related illnesses she acquired as the result of the tension and worry she frequently experienced as a result of her fear of being suffocated. Other medical conditions that have been found to be related to chronic states of anxiety and stress include ulcers, bowel problems, headaches, and backaches.

Feelings While Writing about This Incident

Now take a moment to reflect on the various feelings you had while writing about this incident. Did you feel fear, anger, longing, confusion, self-hate, sexual desire, sexual repulsion, disgust, or a desire for revenge or forgiveness?

If you can't identify any feelings, you need to ask yourself why. Were you truly emotionally neutral or were the feelings so strong or taboo that you need to not remember or feel them? Alternatively, do you feel you would be (or would have been) punished for admitting what those feelings were? If necessary, you may need to consult with a therapist to help you in identifying your feelings.

Managing your fear of engulfment is a process best accomplished step by step, one fear at a time. You have just completed a thorough step-by-step examination of one of the situations that you judged as "Easiest to Handle." After identifying this situation, you then worked on obtaining a better understanding of what happened; the nature of your fear in that situation; your physical reactions; and how your fear affected your behavior, thoughts, and beliefs. This type of in-depth analysis is the first step toward increasing your control in situations that give rise to emotional claustrophobia.

When you feel ready to do more work on your emotional claustrophobia, you can select one or two more incidents from the column "Easiest to Handle." You can use the same instructions to deal with these additional incidents as you used in analyzing the first incident.

Congratulations. You've just done a lot of work. As you continue to gain new insights into this fear, it will begin to lose its power over your ability to love, work, and play.

Chapter 4

Do Your Fears Belong to the Past or the Present?

In chapter 3 you thoroughly examined three instances of emotional claustrophobia. You put each instance under a psychological microscope, examining as many aspects of the incident and as many shifts in your emotional, physical, and mental states as you could remember. The purpose of this intense analysis was to lay the groundwork for finding and putting into effect methods of managing your emotional claustrophobia during similar situations in the future. While you might never feel comfortable in such situations, they need no longer strangle you or fill you with such dread that they restrict your options.

In this chapter, you will take the first steps toward coping with your fear of engulfment. Your first task will be to try to determine some of the possible causes of your emotional claustrophobia for each separate instance. In the following exercise, you can pretend you are a psychologist and analyze how you acquired your fear of engulfment in each separate instance. The causes of your emotional claustrophia may be the same for all three incidents, or they may be different. There may be one central cause, or many causes. Insight into the causes may not be enough to help you manage your fear, but it is an important beginning.

Causes of Your Emotional Claustrophobia

On a fresh page in your journal entitled "Causes of My Emotional Claustrophobia" list the causes of your fear for the three incidents you examined in chapter 3. You should have three such pages, one for each of the three incidents. To help you identify these causes, you may want to review the descriptions of the various causes in chapters 1 and 2, potentially including parental hostility, jealousy, and/or abuse; symbiosis and triangulation in your family of origin; extreme or conflicting expectations; victimization; overpowering personalities; family stress and trauma; difficulties handling certain emotions, such as anger, anxiety, sexuality, and grief. You may also want to review your responses to the self-assessments in chapters 1 and 2.

If you have difficulty identifying the causes of your fear of engulfment, imagine that someone else has the same type of emotional claustrophobia issues as yourself. What would you tell that individual about the causes of his or her fear of engulfment?

How Valid Are the Causes Today?

Some important questions to ask yourself about each of the causes you identified in the previous exercise are: "Is this cause valid today? If so, how valid is it? Is it as valid today as it as in the past?

A situation or individual who was emotionally overwhelming to you in the past may not have the same effect today. If this is the case, you need to make a clear distinction between past and present. If necessary, you will need to remind yourself continually, until it is almost automatic, that what was true in the past is no longer true (or as true) today.

For example, suppose as a child you had a symbiotic relationship with a parent or you were entrapped by parental intrusiveness, jealousy, or triangulation. Now, as an adult, you no longer need your parents for protection and financial support. While it is wonderful to have parental emotional support at any age, as an adult you can find other sources of validation and assistance, and you can also learn to validate yourself. Consequently, if you experience emotional claustrophobia when interacting with your parents in the present—as a result of their past power over you—you need to remind yourself that you are no longer the small child that truly needed and depended on parents for so many aspects of your well-being. You are an independent person now, and while you may still desire to be affirmed, approved of, and assisted by your parents, you can survive without their love and help.

For each of the causes of your emotional claustrophobia, write two or three sentences about whether or not the original power of that cause is still in effect and if so, to what extent?

For example, Annette wrote:

> *The original cause of my fear of engulfment with my mom was that as a child she did engulf me. She took up my time and emotional energy, and she wanted me to share everything with her, even things that children should not have to share with their parents. When friends came over, she would try to make herself part of the conversation. Even when I got married, she interrupted my conversations with my husband to say something. She was so needy I was afraid she would fall apart without me. That's what others told me too—that my mother needed me and that without me, she would become mentally ill. She might have needed me, but I needed her also, because young children are dependent on their parents.*
>
> *How valid is the original cause? I still feel that my mother's intense need of me and her desire to have all of me is a current reality. But the truth is I've been gone from home for over ten years and mom is doing just fine. When I first left home to get married, she yelled and screamed. She even got an ulcer and blamed it on my leaving. She became more depressed that usual, but she didn't land in the hospital or try to commit suicide. My leaving didn't kill her like I thought it would.*
>
> *Also, I don't need her like I used to because I'm an adult now. But I still need her in my life—as an adult daughter needs a mother. And it's okay if she needs me as an adult daughter, too, but not as her rescuer, best friend, or soul mate.*

Tom, who developed fear of engulfment after having worked for an intrusive and controlling manager for ten years, was experiencing fear of engulfment on his new job whenever his new supervisor approached him. When Tom examined the validity of the cause of his emotional claustrophobia in his new job, he wrote:

> *When I was working for Bill, he was at my desk every hour, hounding me for this and complaining about that. He even timed how long I took in the bathroom. He micromanaged me to the point where I felt like I was two years old and a big bad parent was always watching me. Because I needed the paycheck and I felt I didn't have any job options, I tolerated feeling smothered by Bill.*
>
> *My new manager, Andy, is demanding too, but he isn't unreasonable and intrusive like Bill was. Yet whenever Andy*

comes by to check on the status of our project, that old fear of engulfment begins again. But Andy isn't trying to suffocate me. He's only doing his job, even if he is a little authoritarian about it. I need to remind myself that unlike Bill, Andy doesn't direct his anger at me, doesn't ask personal questions, and doesn't come by several times a day—only a few times a week.

The original cause is gone. I really don't have to react with a fear of being smothered anymore. I can be on guard and watch for signs that Andy might become intrusive like Bill, but for now, all I'm dealing with is a demanding boss, not a psychologically disturbed one like Bill. Also, I'm not as financially destitute as I was in the past. Should Andy start turning into a Bill, I can find another job. I may not get paid as much, but now I have an out. I'm not trapped like I was when I was working for Bill.

Action Steps for Certain Causes

Do any of the causes of your fear of engulfment fall into the following categories: ongoing family violence or mistreatment; child abuse or other prior trauma; anger management; anxiety management; overbearing, manipulative, or exploitative individuals; or uncomfortable or distressing sexual arousal? If one or more of the causes of your emotional claustrophobia fit into any of these categories, then take the action steps outlined for each category as follows.

Ongoing Family Violence

If your fear of engulfment stems from ongoing abuse, you need to seek professional and legal help immediately. Review the suggestions in chapter 1 and the appendix for victims of abuse.

Child Abuse or Other Prior Trauma

If your emotional claustrophobia stems from a history of child abuse or some other type of trauma, you need to seek the help of a therapist trained in trauma work. Review the suggestions in chapter 1 for trauma survivors and consult the appendix for recommended reading.

Anger Management

If your fear of engulfment stems from difficulties managing your anger, you need to explore the roots of your anger and, at the very minimum, learn some anger-management techniques. In some cases professional help or medication may be needed, at least in the short-term. Self-help books on anger management are listed in the appendix.

Anxiety Management

If your fear of being smothered is related to problems you have managing your anxiety in numerous situations, not only in situations in which you experience emotional claustrophobia, then you may be suffering from an anxiety or panic disorder for which you will need to consult a trained mental health professional. Some of the available self-help books for anxiety management are listed in the appendix, but you owe it to yourself to get additional professional help.

Overbearing, Manipulative, or Exploitative Individuals

If your fear of engulfment stems from an overbearing, manipulative, or abusive individual with whom you have an unequal power relationship, an exploration of your legal rights and practical alternatives is needed. If this individual is your employer, supervisor, or coworker, then you need to seek assistance from an employee representative or other help available on the job. A consultation with an attorney is also recommended, as is conferring with other employees (or former employees) whom you trust. Depending on the circumstances, you may want to consider job options. Similarly, if your fear of being smothered stems from a domineering roommate, formal negotiations may be needed. If a satisfactory and permanent solution cannot be found, you may need to consider relocation.

For example, Dimitri's college roommate had a drug habit. As the roommate's drug habit worsened, Dimitri's belongings were vandalized and his need for quiet study time was increasingly disregarded. In many ways Dimitri felt trapped by the roommate, and he developed severe emotional claustrophobia as a result. Working on his feelings of engulfment in therapy might have been helpful, but it was not the solution to Dimitri's emotional claustrophobia. He needed to take action.

Dimitri talked to his roommate, then to the roommate's parents, then to college officials. When, for a variety of reasons, it was made clear that the school and the parents were unwilling to remove the roommate from the school dormitory, Dimitri was forced to relocate.

In cases of victimization by external social, military, or political forces or organizations, the psychological techniques described in this book will be of limited effectiveness. For example, suppose you are part of a group and you blow the whistle on corruption within that group. When the expected retaliation comes your way, it may be useful to practice relaxation techniques and other forms of self-soothing and self-calming. However, they will not be enough. Legal, political, and other forms of action will need to be considered.

Sexual Arousal

Sexual arousal in itself is not a cause of emotional claustrophobia, if you are at a level of sexual arousal that feels normal and acceptable to you. However, if some aspect of your level of sexual arousal is uncomfortable to you or feels unacceptable or undesirable, then your sexual arousal can possibly provoke emotional claustrophia. If you have mixed feelings about certain degrees or types of sexual arousal or certain kinds of sex acts, the tension between these conflicting feelings or between your level of physical excitement and your discomfort with that excitement, can leave you feeling overwhelmed and suffocated by your own feelings or your emotional turmoil.

If you have observed that your emotional claustrophobia seems to be related to your sexual feelings or behavior, it will be helpful for you to explore your attitudes and beliefs about sex by taking an inventory of them. This inventory may help you identify those areas of conflict you have about your sexuality, for it is the conflict that can precipitate emotional claustrophobia.

The sex drive is a powerful biological force and the messages you received about sex and sexual conduct were most likely equally powerful. Perhaps the messages you received about sex were mixed or conflicting. Your teachers and religious leaders may have taught you one set of attitudes towards sex; some of your peers, the media, or your sexual partners (if you have been sexually active) may have had different kinds of views.

Many people who have chosen lesbian or gay partners or lifestyles are comfortable with their sexual orientation. However, homosexuality is not universally accepted in our society. Hence some gay men and lesbians find themselves the objects of ridicule, rejection, and abuse. Being attracted to a member of one's own sex is not inherently uncomfortable, however, due to societal prejudice some gay men and lesbians experience anxiety about their sexual orientation. As a result, their erotic impulses may confront them with a dilemma that can feel engulfing, that is, a choice between their true and valid sexual preference and societal pressures to the contrary.

In such situations, being sexually aroused by a member of one's own sex may create an inner conflict that feels engulfing. Even if it were considered desirable, it is not possible to "change" one's sexual orientation to conform to societal expectations. On the other hand, it is very difficult to change entrenched prejudices in certain segments of society, although working toward such change would be a healthy way to direct the tension and anger caused by societal prejudice.

Given the tremendous social and cultural changes in our society and all over the world in recent decades, it is natural and normal for many people to feel confused about sexual issues. A complete guide to dealing with sexuality is beyond the scope of this book. However, one step you can take is to explore your attitudes and beliefs about sex by taking an inventory of them.

Personal Inventory of Sexual Attitudes

On a fresh piece of paper in your journal entitled, "My Feelings about Sex," write six or seven sentences about what you think about sex (in general) and six or sevens sentences about your attitudes toward your (sexuality in particular). Observe how you feel as you reply to these questions. Do you feel anxious, depressed, or angry? Is emotional claustrophobia one of your reactions?

In reviewing what you have written thus far, do you see any relationship between your feelings about sex (in general) or your sexuality (in particular) and your fears about being smothered? Write five or six sentences about the relationship between your sexual attitudes and your emotional claustrophobia, if applicable.

Inventory of Sexual Learnings

Perhaps part of your difficulties with sexual arousal stems from what you learned about sex from other people: what they told you about sex and what you observed about how they conducted their sex lives. The following inventory may help you uncover the roots of some of the emotional claustrophobia you may experience related to your sexuality.

On a fresh piece of paper in your journal entitled "Messages about Sex," answer the following questions to the best of your ability. Divide the piece of paper into two columns. In the first column, answer the question, "What did the following people or groups tell me about sex?" In the second column, answer the question, "What did this same person or group teach me about sex by the way they handled their own sexuality?"

What I Was Told about Sex	**What I Learned about Sex from Observing This Person or Group**
Mother	
Father	
Brother(s)	
Sister(s)	
Grandparents	
Aunts/Uncles	
Cousins/Other family members	
Step- or foster parent	
Step- or foster siblings	
Other step-family members	
Childhood religious group	
Other religious groups	
Friends (pre-adolescent)	
Friends (adolescent)	
Friends (adult)	
Current friends	
Former employer/coworkers	
Current employer/coworkers	
Former sexual partners (if applicable)	
Current sexual partner or mate (if applicable)	

Review what you have written in the chart above. Are there any contradictions between what certain people or groups told you about sex and how they behaved sexually? Make a list of these contradictions.

Now review your sexual learnings inventory once more. Were there any contradictions or differences between what one person or group told you about sex and what another person or group stated to you? If so, what are these contradictions?

Do any of the differences or contradictions you have listed above have a direct bearing on your own attitudes toward your sexuality? If so, write five or six sentences addressing this issue.

Do you feel clear and firm on where you stand on issues related to sex? If not, in which areas do you feel conflicted, unsure or confused? Is your fear of suffocation somehow related to these areas of confusion? For example, if you are unsure about whether you feel it is right to engage in premarital or extramarital sex and are then presented with an opportunity to do so, your sexual arousal may feel engulfing. Aside from any other factors involved, such as the appropriateness of your sex partner, any confusion you have about what is appropriate sexual behavior may contribute to feeling suffocated by your sexual arousal.

If you experience emotional claustrophobia when sexually aroused, is there any relationship between what you have been taught about sex and your emotional claustrophobia? For example, were you ever told that it was wrong to be sexually aroused by a relative, to be aroused by a member of your own sex, or to be aroused on a daily basis? Do you believe that sexual arousal in itself is dangerous or undesirable under almost all circumstances or are only certain types of sexual arousal to be disdained and avoided?

For example, Robin considered herself a happily married woman. She had never strayed sexually in her marriage. One night she met a distant cousin of her husband's whom she had never met before. She was instantly and powerfully attracted to him. For weeks afterwards, Robin experienced bouts of emotional claustrophobia whenever she thought about meeting that cousin, whenever her husband mentioned the cousin's name, and whenever she went to bed with her husband.

Robin's emotional claustrophobia was not rooted in any uncertainties about her sexual standards: she clearly felt that extramarital sex was wrong. Neither was it rooted in being afraid of being sexually aroused. Robin accepted her sexual arousal, even being sexually aroused by other men. But she felt that being attracted to a family member, even if it was not a blood relative and was someone whom she had never met before, was morally deranged. Somewhere in her upbringing she had been told that persons with desires like hers were depraved and would be punished.

Still other questions to be considered in assessing the role of sexual feelings and attitudes in your emotional claustrophobia are the following:

Does your fear of being suffocated stem from your being afraid you won't be able to control yourself once you become sexually aroused? Being sexually aroused and acting on that arousal are different, just as feeling angry at someone and actually assaulting them are different. How clear is that difference for you?

Reviewing the chart you completed above, were there people in your life who were unable to control their sexual behavior? Was this ever the case with you? Do you have a history of being unable to control yourself after becoming sexually aroused? Is it possible that your emotional claustrophobia is related to any fears you might have about being able to control yourself sexually?

If so, are you concerned that you might put yourself in emotionally damaging or physically harmful situations as the result of your difficulties restraining your sexual behavior? If this is the case, you need to seek professional help.

Chapter 5

Managing Your
Anxiety

The techniques presented in this chapter include some of the standard methods therapists have used for many decades to help people calm themselves and reduce the physiological effects of various types of fears. These techniques include deep breathing, muscle relaxation, eye relaxation, and creating a safe place. The possible benefits of physical exercise are also discussed.

These methods, as well as others, have helped countless people stop the vicious cycle of emotional claustrophobia that make you feel out of control and helpless and that causes the emotional claustrophobia to grow by leaps and bounds. By using these or other methods of self-soothing and calming, you can prevent an initial surge of emotional claustrophobia from growing to the point where it dominates your being.

Chapter 6 will help you manage your thinking processes so that they reflect present, not past, realities and options. After you complete these two chapters, you will have learned two basic skills for managing your fear of engulfment: how to take charge of your body and how to take charge of the beliefs that control your mind.

How Anxiety Can Affect Your Physical and Mental Powers

Part of the hell of suffering from fear of engulfment is that it leads to yet another fear: the fear that you will lose control of yourself. Most people, when they become extremely afraid or anxious, experience problems functioning mentally. They tend to overreact or underreact, and thinking straight, remembering, organizing, and reacting appropriately become difficult, if not impossible. Larry, a forty-five-year-old physics professor explains:

> *I get stupid. If something sets off my fear of engulfment, my mind slows down. I can't answer simple questions and I feel confused. People look at me as if my IQ just dropped fifty points. If the fear hits while I'm lecturing, then completing sentences and going from one thought to another become monumental tasks. Students ask me to repeat a point and I can't remember what I just said. A couple of times I've snapped back at students, calling them "slow" or "stupid" for asking me to repeat something. But the truth is that once that fear of engulfment starts, I'm the one who is slow and stupid.*

To help himself, Larry types his lecture notes and distributes them to his students. That way when a student asks for clarification, Larry can refer to his written handout, which for him, in a state of fear, is much easier than trying to think of what to say.

If you are like Larry, past experience may have taught you once the fear of engulfment invades your psyche, you begin to have memory problems, or you might say or do things you regret or fail to do or say what you intended to. You might also start perspiring, shaking, or having other physical reactions that make you self-conscious and cause you embarrassment. These reactions, like Larry's "getting stupid" reaction, are all normal responses to fear and severe anxiety. Both the physical reactions, like perspiring, and the mental reactions, like having trouble remembering, are due to increase in the flow of adrenaline and other biochemical changes in the body that occur when a person feels threatened or trapped. (See chapter 3 for a more detailed description of some of the mental consequences of emotional claustrophobia.)

Imagine yourself beginning to experience fear of engulfment. As you feel the tension rising within you, you begin to panic because you are afraid that once the fear begins, there is no stopping it. You wonder (and legitimately so) if the fear will escalate to unbearable proportions and render you helpless and powerless.

However, if you know you have ways of calming and centering yourself, you will have weapons with which to combat the rising fear. You may not be able to eliminate the fear entirely. But if you are prepared with ways of calming yourself, you can assure yourself that you can *manage* your fear reactions *sufficiently to cope with the situation at hand.*

Your Physical Reactions to Fear

In chapter 3, you described three instances of fear of engulfment in detail, including your physical reactions. Look over what you have written in response to the question on your physical and bodily reactions to your fear in the inventory you completed in chapter 3. Based on what you have written, where in your body do you tend to feel the fear?

Techniques for Managing Anxiety

The areas where you tend to feel the fear are the areas you need to focus on as you experiment with different methods of reducing the physical effects of anxiety. These methods include muscle relaxation, eye relaxation, breathing control, physical exercise, and creating a safe place. As you try out each of these methods, you may find one or more of them useful. The more ways you have to calm yourself, the better. Due to space limitations, other methods of self-calming, such as meditation, self-hypnosis, biofeedback, and autogenics are not presented here. You can learn about these methods in *The Relaxation and Stress Reduction Workbook*, Fifth Edition, by Martha Davis, Elizabeth Eschelman, and Matthew Mc Kay (2000) and other books on anxiety management listed in the appendix.

The Importance of Practice

In order to benefit from these methods, you need to practice them repeatedly until they become almost automatic. It is not enough to simply read about them or have an intellectual understanding of these exercises. You have to *do* them and they have to become a *habit*. Every time you practice one of these exercises, you are training your body to listen to your mind so that when your start becoming afraid, instead of automatically becoming more afraid, your mind will automatically instruct your body, "relax your muscles" or "do your breathing exercises," and your body will obey.

The breathing and muscle relaxation exercises presented here are relatively simple and can be easily learned. But this does not mean that you can instantly remember them when you need them. When you are in a situation you find threatening, your initial reaction of fear may have already impaired your thinking abilities so that you forget that these methods even exist. All too often my clients have stated, "I was so afraid at the time that I forgot about taking a few deep breaths or doing the muscle relaxation exercises. I guess I should have practiced them. Then I would have remembered."

Beth first learned how to manage severe anxiety in her natural childbirth classes when she was preparing to have her first child. In childbirth classes pregnant women learn to relax during labor through a variety of techniques, including deep breathing and visualizing a safe or pleasant place (which will be described later in this chapter). These techniques not only help the woman relax (as much as is humanly possible during childbirth), but also help to lessen the pain because pain usually feels greater when a person is tense.

When Beth's labor began, she felt smothered both physically and emotionally. She was so afraid and in so much pain she felt sure she would not be able to breathe as she had been taught, even though she had practiced many hours. Much to Beth's amazement, her body easily followed her mental command to breathe a certain way. Controlling her breathing helped her feel more confident and helped to reduce her physical sensation of pain. Beth explains:

> I wasn't a model breather. Several times I gave in to the panic and my pain got worse. Yet the minute I told myself that I'd better do some of those breathing exercises, my body responded almost immediately—and automatically. Not only did my feelings of being smothered lessen, but my pain lessened as well. It's a good thing I practiced a lot because with all the pain and emotional claustrophobia I had during labor, I would have never remembered even the simplest breathing exercise. Even with my husband by my side coaching me, if I hadn't practiced daily for months, I would have been hard-pressed to breathe in ways that would help me.

Maria had a similar success experience as the result of practice. In her journal she wrote:

> I just got over a bout of fear of engulfment. Wow, what a term! I must be doing my psychological homework to even be thinking in terms like "fear of engulfment." While I was driving home I began being afraid of being smothered. "What now? What am I so scared of?" I asked myself.

> *After a few moments of panicked thought, I realized that*
> *I feared going home because then I would see my husband. I felt*
> *that if he said even one word to me I would feel suffocated or*
> *disappear. I was afraid that I'd yell at him or just say nothing*
> *and act like a zombie, hoping he wouldn't notice me. I thought*
> *of a dozen reasons to avoid him, like telling him I had the flu or*
> *that I needed to take a nap. I needed breathing room and I was*
> *willing to lie to get it.*
>
> *I was so tense driving I could hardly think. It was an*
> *effort to drive carefully. "I don't want to live like this ... feeling*
> *smothered just thinking of my husband and planning how to*
> *tune out of life and not be present," I thought to myself. Then*
> *somehow I remembered to do a few deep breathing and relaxation*
> *exercises.*
>
> *I really don't believe in all that muscle relaxation and*
> *breathing stuff, but I had practiced muscle relaxation and deep*
> *breathing exercises a lot in order to please my therapist. But for*
> *some reason, despite my skepticism, I told my muscles to relax.*
> *I didn't have the patience to relax each muscle, like I was taught,*
> *and I only took one deep breath, instead of several like the*
> *therapist said I was supposed to.*
>
> *I really didn't believe that telling my muscles to relax,*
> *which only took a few seconds, would make any difference, but it*
> *did. I didn't get calm, but I calmed down enough to realize what*
> *the problem was. I had sexual desire and was afraid that if I gave*
> *into it and approached my husband, he would be frightened by the*
> *intensity of my desire and then reject me because he tends to be*
> *sexually reserved. I was also afraid of my desire because if I give*
> *into it, I might spend more time lovemaking and less time being*
> *productive, which is threatening to me because people value me,*
> *and I value myself, for all the projects I complete and all the help*
> *I give others. Once I knew what the problem was, I could deal*
> *with it. I was so relieved that it was desire I was feeling and not*
> *that there was some major problem between me and my husband.*

As Beth's and Maria's stories illustrate, the more you practice
the exercises, the more they will become a part of you. Think of how
many times you have practiced becoming more and more afraid!
You are probably an expert at how to make yourself feel smothered.
Now you need to become an expert at another process—centering
and calming yourself.

If you practice these exercises in nonthreatening situations, then
when you are under fire, you will be more likely to recall and use
them. Another benefit of frequent practice is that repeated use of
these techniques over time can actually produce changes in your

brain chemistry that can reduce the physiological effects of fear and help you take charge of fearful situations (Zuercher-White 1998).

If you have not read the introduction to this book, please do so with special attention to the cautions for trauma survivors before trying the exercises in this chapter. Many studies have shown the positive effects of muscle relaxation, meditation, and other calming techniques. However, a few studies have shown that for some people, meditation and muscle relaxation techniques produced negative effects, such as increased anxiety, withdrawal, confusion, and restlessness (Smith 1998).

Always judge the effectiveness of any technique by its outcome. Does the technique help, even a little? You cannot expect any technique to totally eliminate your anxiety and tension, but if it reduces your anxiety and stress to a manageable level or to a point where the fear doesn't interfere with your reasoning powers, then it can be considered useful.

Deep Breathing

Your degree of body tension is reflected in the way you breathe. When you are under stress, you breathe shallowly. Conversely, you can learn to calm yourself by practicing deep breathing exercises. Deep breathing increases the oxygen flow to your brain, which increases your capacity to think and concentrate and helps rid your body of toxins.

The following exercises will be useful to you not only in dealing with situations in which you experience fear of engulfment, but also in other efforts and in any life circumstance in which you want or need to calm yourself. Two forms of deep breathing exercises are offered here: abdominal breathing and calming breath (Bourne 2000).

Try to practice one of the following techniques regularly. Five minutes a day for two weeks is recommended. Once you've become comfortable with one of the forms, you use it to combat stress, anxiety, and emotional claustrophobia.

Continuing to practice either of these techniques will make it second nature. You will naturally breathe more deeply, which will promote feelings of relaxation and well-being.

Every time we have an emotion such as fear, a cascade of neurochemicals is released through our body, some of which directly affect our health. For example, our limbic system, the emotional center of our brain, is linked to the part of our brain that controls our heart rate. Repeated stimulation of this part of the brain due to intense negative emotions and stress can lead to cardiac arrest and other heart problems. So can repeated surges of adrenaline, which are triggered by danger, ordinary stress, or fears, such as fear of being smothered or suffocated. Just taking a few deep breaths sends electrical signals to your brain to relax your muscles, which can reduce your blood pressure and the stress on your heart, as well as improve your ability to focus and think clearly.

Abdominal Breathing Exercises

1. Note the level of tension you're feeling. Then place one hand on your abdomen right beneath your rib cage.

2. Inhale slowly and deeply through your nose into the "bottom" of you lungs—in other words, send the air as low down as you can. When you're breathing from your abdomen, your hand should actually rise. Your chest should move only slightly while your abdomen expands. (In abdominal breathing, the diaphragm—the muscle that separates the lung cavity from the abdominal cavity—moves downward, causing the muscles surrounding the abdominal cavity to push outward.)

3. When you've taken in a full breath, pause for a moment, and then exhale slowly through your nose or mouth, depending on your preference. Be sure to exhale fully. As you exhale, allow your whole body to just let go. (You might visualize your arms and legs going loose and limp like a rag doll's.)

4. Do ten slow, full abdominal breaths. Try to keep your breathing smooth and regular, without gulping in a big breath all at once. Remember to pause briefly at the end of each inhalation. Count to ten, progressing with each exhalation. The process should go like this:

   Slow . . . inhale . . . Pause . . . Slow exhale (count one)

   Slow . . . inhale . . . Pause . . . Slow exhale (count two)

   Slow . . . inhale . . . Pause . . . Slow exhale (count three) (and so on up to ten). If you start to feel light-headed while practicing abdominal breathing, stop for thirty seconds, and then start up again.

5. Extend the exercise if you wish by doing two or three "sets" of abdominal breaths, remembering to count up to ten for each set (each exhalation counts as one number). Five full minutes of abdominal breathing will have a pronounced effect in reducing anxiety or early symptoms of panic.

If you prefer to count backwards from ten down to one on each breath. Feel free to do so.

Calming Breath Exercise

1. Breathing from your abdomen, inhale slowly to a count of five (count slowly "one ... two ... three ... four ... five" as you inhale).

2. Pause and hold your breath to a count of five.

3. Exhale slowly, through your nose or mouth, to a count of five (or more if it takes you longer). Be sure to exhale fully.

4. When you've exhaled completely, take two breaths in your normal rhythm, then repeat steps one through three in the cycle above.

5. Keep up the exercise for at least five minutes. This should involve going through at least ten cycles of in-five, hold-five, out-five. Remember to take two normal breaths between each cycle. If you start to feel light-headed while practicing this exercise, stop for thirty seconds and then start again.

6. Throughout the exercise, keep up breathing smooth and regular, without gulping in breaths or breathing out suddenly.

7. Optional: Each time you exhale you may wish to say "relax," "calm," "let go," or any other relaxing word or phrase silently to yourself. Allow your whole body to let go as you do this.

Progressive Muscle Relaxation

Muscle tension that is prolonged due to stress or trauma can hinder circulation and create fatigue. Our body consists of 620 skeletal muscles. When they contract, glycogen is broken down, which creates lactic acid, which leads to fatigue (Smith 1998).

The progressive muscle relaxation technique developed over fifty years ago by Dr. Edmund Jacobson has been shown to reverse the negative side effects of muscle tension caused by stress. It can also help you achieve a means of relaxing in the midst of stress, such as while feeling the fear of engulfment. This technique can be especially effective if you feel anxiety physically, in the form of tightness in your neck, shoulders, back, jaw, or around your eyes, or if you experience high blood pressure, insomnia, muscle spasms, or headaches associated with tension.

Progressive muscle relaxation involves tensing and then relaxing sixteen different muscle groups. It takes only fifteen to twenty minutes to do, and requires nothing more than quiet and enough space to comfortably sit or lie down. Unless you experience overwhelming negative thoughts during the exercise, or unless some of the muscles being used have been injured so that the exercise is painful, there should be no reason you cannot use this relaxation technique.

Here are a few general guidelines:

- Set aside enough time (you might need thirty minutes at first) each day for doing the exercises. When you first get up, before going to bed, and before a meal are the best times. After eating is the worst.

- Make sure you're comfortable; the room should be a comfortable temperature, quiet, and free from interruptions; your clothing should not be restrictive; and your entire body needs to be supported. You can lie down, perhaps with a pillow beneath your knees for support. Or you can sit in a chair, but be sure your head is supported along with the rest of your body. (Sitting may be preferable if you feel unsafe lying down because of past trauma. Whenever and however you position yourself, be sure you feel safe.)

- Try not to worry or think about outside events. Put them away for the time being. Also, don't worry about your performance of the technique. You are not at work or on a sports team where you are competing with others. Your goal is relaxation.

Aside from helping you cope with trigger situations, regular, daily practice of progressive muscle relaxation can have a significant beneficial effect on your general anxiety level. You can also use the following exercises (from Bourne 2000) before, during, or after completing any of the written exercises in this book.

The idea is to tense each muscle group hard (but not so hard that you strain) for about ten seconds, and then to let go of it suddenly. Your then give yourself fifteen to twenty seconds to relax, noticing how the muscle group feels when relaxed in contrast to how it felt when tensed, before going on to the next group of muscles. You might also say to yourself "I am relaxing," "let go," "let the tension flow away," or any other relaxing phrase during each relaxation period between successive muscle groups. Throughout the exercise, maintain your focus on your muscles. When your attention wanders, bring it back to the particular muscle group you're working on. The following guidelines describe progressive muscle relaxation in detail:

- When you tense a particular muscle, do so vigorously, without straining, for seven to ten seconds. You may want to count "one-thousand-one," "one-thousand-two," and so on, as a way of marking off seconds.

- Concentrate on what is happening. Feel the buildup of tension in each particular muscle group. It is often helpful to visualize the particular muscle group being tensed.

- When you release the muscles, do so abruptly, and then relax, enjoying the sudden feeling of limpness. Allow the relaxation to develop for at least fifteen to twenty seconds before going on the next group of muscles.

- Allow all the *other* muscles in your body to remain relaxed, as far as possible, while working on a particular muscle group.

- Tense and relax each muscle group once. But if a particular area feels especially tight, you can tense and relax it two or three times, waiting about twenty seconds between each cycle.

Once you are comfortably supported in a quiet place, follow these detailed instructions.

1. To begin, take three abdominal breaths, exhaling slowly each time. As you exhale, imagine that tension throughout your body is beginning to flow away.

2. Clench your fists. Hold seven to ten seconds, and then release for fifteen to twenty seconds. Use these same time intervals for all other muscle groups.

3. Tighten your biceps by drawing your forearms up toward your shoulders and "making a muscle" with both arms. Hold, and then relax.

4. Tighten your triceps—the muscles on the undersides of your upper arms—by extending your arms out straight and locking your elbows. Hold, and then relax.

5. Tense the muscles in your forehead by raising your eyebrows as far as you can. Hold, and then relax. Imagine your forehead muscles becoming smooth and limp as they relax.

6. Tense the muscles around your eyes by clenching your eyelids tightly shut. Hold, and then relax. Imagine sensations of deep relaxation spreading all around the area of your eyes.

7. Tighten your jaws by opening your mouth so widely that you stretch the muscles around the hinges of your jaw. Hold, and then relax. Let your lips part and allow your jaw to hang loose.

8. Tighten the muscles in the back of your neck by pulling your head back, as if you were going to touch your head to your back. (Be gentle with this muscle group to avoid injury.) Focus only on tensing the muscles in your neck. Hold, and then relax. Since this area is often especially tight, it's good to do the tense/relax sequence twice.

9. Take a few deep breaths and tune in to the weight of your head sinking into whatever surface it is resting on.

10. Tighten your shoulders by raising them up as if you were going to touch your ears. Hold, then relax.

11. Tighten the muscles around your shoulder blades by pushing your shoulder blades back as if you were going to touch them together. Hold the tension in your shoulder blades, and then relax. Since this area is often especially tense, you might repeat the tense/relax sequence twice.

12. Tighten the muscles of your chest by taking in a deep breath. Hold for up to ten seconds, and then release slowly. Imagine any excess tension in your chest flowing away with the exhalation.

13. Tighten your stomach muscles by sucking in your stomach. Hold, and then release. Imagine a wave of relaxation spreading through your abdomen.

14. Tighten your lower back by arching it up. (You can omit this exercise if you have lower back pain.) Hold, and then relax.

15. Tighten your buttocks by pulling them together. Hold, and then relax. Imagine the muscles in your hips going loose and limp.

16. Squeeze the muscles in your thighs all the way down to your knees. (You will probably have to tighten your hips along with your thighs, since the thigh muscles attach at the pelvis.) Hold, and then relax. Feel your thigh muscles smoothing out and relaxing completely.

17. Tighten your calf muscles by pulling your toes toward you. (Flex carefully to avoid cramps.) Hold, and then relax.

18. Tighten you feet by curling your toes downward. Hold, and them relax.

19. Mentally scan your body for any residual tension. If a particular area remains tense, repeat one or two tense/relax sequences for that group of muscles.

20. Now imagine a wave of relaxation spreading slowly throughout your body, starting at your head and gradually penetrating every muscle group all the way down to your toes.

You might want to record the above exercises on an audiocassette to expedite your early practice sessions. Or you may wish to obtain a professionally made tape of the progressive muscle relaxation exercise. There are many of these available, some of which are to be played while you sleep. However, the sleep tapes have not been proven to be particularly effective, and are additionally not practical for those who have trouble sleeping. Information on audiotapes and other books and other materials on relaxation are listed in the appendix.

Eye Relaxation

Another relaxation technique, which takes less time to learn and use, is the eye relaxation technique (Davis et al. 2000). The eye relaxation technique involves closing your eyes and gently placing the palms of your hand over your eyes. Your goal is to block out the light without putting pressure on your eyelids. Then imagine the color black. Other colors and images may float into your mind, but focus on this color. You might want to use a mental image, such as a black suitcase, black coat, or another black object to keep your mind focused on that color.

After two or three minutes, open your eyes slowly and gradually. As your eyes open, you should experience relaxation in your eye muscles.

Physical Exercise

For some people, meditation and relaxation are counterproductive. For them, focused energy in the form of physical activity is helpful. Activities that involve physical exertion, for example, walking, swimming, jogging and aerobic dance, are highly recommended for dealing with fears and anxieties. Gardening, woodcarving, and other types of activities can also be helpful.

Exercise is a proven method of stress reduction. Not only does it help to release anger and anxiety, but it also stimulates the production of endorphins and other antidepressants in the brain. Unless medically contraindicated, exercise is an excellent way to improve mental health (Mc Kay et. al. 1989).

Numerous books and programs are available to help you get started on a course of aerobic exercise. It need not be expensive or complex—walking can be one of the best forms of exercise there is, if it's done right. Just keep a few things in mind:

- Be sure to obtain your physician's approval before you begin any type of exercise program.

- Don't start too strenuously or abruptly. Get a checkup and talk to your doctor about what you propose to do. This is especially important if you smoke, are sedentary, have a family history of medical problems, or have existing medical conditions of your own.

- Warm up before and cool down after exercise. Allow at least five minutes of stretching and light exercise before and after your activity.

- At all times, pay attention to your body. If it screams "stop!" then stop. Warning signs include hyperventilation, chest pain, inability to breathe, or any form of pain or acute discomfort (McKay et al. 1989).

Creating a Safe Place

Can you visualize or imagine a safe place in your mind? Perhaps there was some place as a child where you felt safe from harm and free to be yourself, without fear of being criticized, controlled, or harmed by others. If there was no such place in your past, is there a physical place right now in your life, which is comfortable, peaceful, and safe?

Close your mind and imagine this place. It needs to be a place that you control and where you only allow those persons, objects, or pets that are a comfort to you, that inspire you, and that affirm your worth. Therefore, your safe place has to have an entrance that only you can control.

As you imagine your safe place, put in physical details, such as the size and color of the room and the types of objects in the room. Go into that safe place and touch the various objects. Smell the air— what do you smell? Where do you sit or rest in your safe place? Imagine yourself sitting comfortable there. Who or what else is with you? How does their presence comfort and please you?

Spend a few minutes visualizing your safe place. It may be a real place or a fantasy. In either case, tell yourself that you can go to this safe place, mentally, at any time. When you are stressed, you can take yourself to your safe place in your mind, rest there surrounded by your safety zone, and figure out how best to handle any current challenge.

Medication

If the methods suggested in this chapter fail to help you, or are only partially effective, you may want to consider medication. Arrange for a consultation with a psychiatrist to consider the option of any variety of medications that have brought relief to many who suffer from severe anxiety and tension. Some people have found that they needed antianxiety medication to help them through a difficult period but were able to do without it once their life circumstances had stabilized. Some medications must be taken regularly; others, only as needed.

There are many antianxiety medications or minor tranquilizers available. Many are relatively safe and have relatively few side effects. However, medication is a short-term solution to stress and fear of engulfment. Being able to calm yourself through relaxation or breathing exercises or by some other technique and by reminding yourself of your true capabilities in any situation are necessary for long-term control of physical tension. (Caution: If you do begin taking psychiatric medications, consult with your doctor before you attempt any of the relaxation and other exercises described in this chapter.)

Chapter 6

Taking Charge of
Your Mind: Evaluating
Your Beliefs

In this chapter, you will become more sharply aware of the beliefs
you hold when you are in the grips of fear of engulfment. After you
identify your beliefs, you will be asked to question them by asking
yourself: To what extent are these beliefs true? How useful are these
beliefs in promoting my well-being and the well-being of others? To
what extent do my beliefs need to be modified?

Some of your beliefs may not need to be totally discarded, they
may simply need to be altered or modified to reflect the facts of the
situation: that is, the truth about you, the other person, and your real
options.

How Thoughts and
Feelings Relate

One of the most popular and effective forms of therapy today is
called cognitive therapy. This type therapy is based on the fact that
our cognition, that is, what we think and believe, can greatly affect

the way we feel and act. But cognitive therapy is not a form of mind-control or rationalization. It's purpose is not to have you "think away" your feelings. For example, it wouldn't be effective to use cognitive therapy to avoid feeling grief over the death of a loved one. Cognitive therapy could help you view the loss realistically, but it could never erase the pain of a major loss.

Similarly, cognitive therapy cannot eliminate the anxiety and fear you feel in certain situations. However, by viewing the situation accurately and realistically, you may reduce or eliminate fears which are grounded in past, not present, realities, or in false and limiting beliefs you hold about yourself and your options. When our beliefs are accurate, we function effectively. However, if our beliefs are inaccurate, incomplete, inflexible, or otherwise not right for the situation at hand, we may suffer needlessly.

Challenging Untrue Beliefs

Some of the beliefs you hold about yourself may be accurate and realistic; others may not be. For example, some people suffer from the unrealistic idea that they are powerless, worthless, inept, unlovable, weak, or unable to fend for themselves or take care of themselves. If you hold these beliefs, such beliefs need to be refuted. For example:

Belief: I am powerless.

Rebuttal: Unless you are being held captive in a traumatic situation, you are never *totally* powerless. There is always *something* you can do for yourself to improve the situation, even if it is breathing deeply, visualizing your safe place, or getting a drink of water.

Belief: I am worthless or unlovable.

Rebuttal: If you felt you were *totally* worthless or unlovable, you would not have purchased this book. Even if you suffer from feelings of low self-worth, some small part of you must consider yourself worthwhile or you would not have invested the energy to read this book and work on these exercises.

Suppose you do feel unlovable, and deeply so. This feeling can not be easily swept away no matter who tries to convince you otherwise. However, the fact that you are spending time trying to deal with your fear of engulfment so that you can have a better life shows that at least one person, you (or a part of you), cares about you. The self-loving part of you may need to grow, but the basis for developing healthy self-love, the wish to feel worthy and good about oneself, is already present. If it did not exist, you wouldn't be reading this paragraph.

(Note: Persistent feelings of worthlessness are a symptom of clinical depression. Talk to a mental health professional if your feelings of worthlessness are reoccurring or are immobilizing you. If you suffer from clinical depression, you may need medication and other forms of help to combat such feelings.)

Belief: I'm not strong or capable enough to express myself or take care of my needs.

Rebuttal: If you feel weak or insecure about taking care of yourself or asserting yourself, it may be true that you need to be strengthened in these areas. However, it is inaccurate to think you are *totally* unable to take care of yourself or that you can *never* learn how to be more self-protective, assertive, or self-nurturing. You bought this book as a beginning toward empowering yourself and perhaps you have made other efforts toward self-improvement. The appendix lists additional books that can help you in this process, and you can also help yourself by seeking individual and group therapy or by getting involved in a recovery or self-help program.

While you may think of yourself as "weak" for having a problem like emotional claustrophobia, recognizing that you have this problem and being willing to take action to deal with it in a healthy way are signs of strength. It takes strength—and courage—to be honest with oneself, to take responsibility for one's thoughts and behavior, and to be open to the possibility of change. Just look around you. How many people do you know who are willing to go through the pain of self-examination and the work of trying to figure out better ways of handling certain situations?

The belief that you are weak or incompetent cannot be accurate unless you are ineffective in *every* area of life *all the time*. It's virtually impossible to be incompetent in *every* dimension of living *every single moment* of your life. Taking pride in, or at least acknowledging, the things you are competent in (i.e., loving your pet, driving a car, having the courage to read this book) can help you start to address your feelings of low self-worth).

Reading this book and thinking about your difficulties with emotional claustrophobia requires discipline, commitment, and focus, as well as the ability to try to see yourself and others clearly, to think analytically and creatively, and to learn new skills. These are hardly the traits of a "weak" person: they are traits held by people with a high potential to be innovative and highly functioning.

Confronting your emotional claustrophobia, trying to be effective in situations that are smothering to you, and trying to solve relationship problems with people who you are afraid might stifle you requires considerable intelligence. Dealing with the many internal struggles involved in coping with emotional claustrophobia and with the issues involved in negotiating relationships can be as complex and sensitive a matter as the inner workings of a computer.

To a great degree, we are not responsible for our beliefs about ourselves, others, and the world. We learned our beliefs from our family of origin, our teachers and friends, our employers and coworkers, the media, and other important influences in our life. These beliefs are not necessarily wrong or mistaken, but they are not automatically right or helpful just because someone you loved and respected or someone or something that had power over you taught you these beliefs.

In *Prisoners of Belief* Matthew McKay and Patrick Fanning (1991) help people identify and critically examine certain core beliefs that significantly shape their lives. McKay and Fanning note that our core beliefs tend to center about ten themes: value, security, performance, control, love, autonomy, justice, belonging, trusting others, and standards. Your core beliefs about your value (how valuable you think you are), competence (how capable you think you are), lovableness (how lovable you feel you are), and autonomy (how independent you feel and how much you can trust yourself to take care of yourself) may come to the fore as you examine the beliefs you hold while experiencing fear of engulfment.

Guidance in assessing your views of yourself and your core beliefs about your worthiness and lovableness are beyond the scope of this book. For further help in these areas, consult books under the category "Self-Esteem and Assertiveness" in the appendix.

Identifying Your Self-Defeating Beliefs

Your first task is to make a list of the beliefs you held during each incident you listed in chapter 3. On a fresh sheet in your journal entitled "My Beliefs," draw a line down the middle of the page. Entitle the first column "My Beliefs" and the second, "Evaluation." In the first column, list the beliefs you held during each incident. There should be a separate sheet for each incident.

Your beliefs are fundamental to every aspect of your being. Yet if you are like many others, you may not be familiar with the beliefs that exert so much control over your life. Many people operate on the basis of their beliefs automatically, as if pulled by invisible strings. The purpose of this exercise is to make your invisible strings visible. The more you write and think about the underlying beliefs you experience during your fear of engulfment, the sharper the awareness of your beliefs and the greater the possibility that you will continue to discover additional beliefs. You will then be in a better position to identify the beliefs that limit your options or that are not relevant to the situation.

What Is Your Body Saying?

One way to help you uncover additional beliefs is to consider the parts of your body that tend to react strongly to fear of engulfment. If these parts of your body could talk, what would they say?

Asking this question is not meant to imply that your mind is creating your physical distress; that is, that your physical pain or other symptoms are "all in your head." Your physical distresses are real and all the thinking and wishing you can muster may not make them diminish or disappear. However, using your imagination to view these physical symptoms as possible expressions of emotional pain may be a useful way of getting in touch with your thoughts and feelings.

For example, nausea is a common response to anxiety and stress, but this does not mean that if you become nauseated when you're anxious that you chose or willed yourself to have this problem. When you are stressed due to fear, your blood is channeled away from the internal organs toward the larger muscles in the arms and legs. This change in blood flow, which contributes to feelings of nausea, is an automatic physiological response designed to prepare you for the mobility necessary to flee, fight, or take some other action necessary for survival. Under conditions of danger (or possible danger), it is more important that you be able to run fast than it is to digest your food.

Even if your nausea is basically an involuntary physiological response to fear, not a self-chosen reaction, you may still be able to learn something about yourself by asking, "If my stomach could talk, what would it say?" The purpose of asking this type of question is to help you gain insight into your emotions and beliefs, not to make you feel responsible or guilty for your physical problems.

Len experienced a fear of engulfment and nausea during his yearly job evaluation. Evaluations tend to make many people somewhat anxious, but Len's anxiety escalated to the point where he felt he was going to be engulfed. Len's intense reaction was rooted in his military experience: as the result of a negative training evaluation, he was sent to the front lines.

When asked what his stomach would say if it could talk, Len wrote:

"I'm very afraid that if don't measure up, I might die or get fired. I'm doing the best job possible, but I still don't measure up. I'm helpless. There's nothing I can do to improve my performance or stop this man from making decisions that might kill me. I feel like throwing up because I can't stand the thought of dying. I'm angry too: it isn't my fault I'm not superman. Nobody's perfect, but how many people get sent to a war zone because they got a B+ instead of an A– on a practice drill?"

In listening to his stomach "talk" Leonard recognized three of his underlying beliefs: (1)"If I don't make the grade, I'm incompetent and worthless," (2) "My own failings are the cause of my anxiety. If I get fired, it's because I'm inept," and (3) "There's no use trying because you have to be perfect or almost perfect to succeed." He also realized that these beliefs were not entirely accurate and that he was confusing his present situation, which wasn't life-threatening, with his military experience, which truly had been life-threatening.

The War Within

Another way to help you identify your beliefs is to consider the possibility that you harbor a "war within," that is, that you hold two opposing beliefs or that you are torn between two important commitments or emotional attachments. Quite often emotional claustrophobia can also arise from a clash between two or more powerful loves or values within yourself. This can lead to severe anxiety when it seems, or actually is, impossible to choose between them, especially when a choice is necessary or seems necessary.

Roberto's Story

Roberto, an engineer, felt smothered when presented with a golden job opportunity. The job offered him the challenge and salary he had been working toward for years. But taking the job meant going overseas for at least six months, perhaps even longer. Roberto was told that every high level employee was expected "do time in the boonies" and that if he accepted this project he would never be asked to leave his family again. The additional income would help pay for Roberto's son's physical therapy and his wife's tuition. On the other hand, Roberto dreaded the long separation and the emotional and sexual deprivation it would imply.

At first Roberto tried to approach this decision logically, by making a pros and cons list. But just picking up a pencil to make the list resulted in feelings of suffocation so strong he had to put the pencil down. When he tried to talk about it with his wife, he felt so suffocated he changed the subject. In desperation, he called a therapist, but the day of the first appointment, he canceled. As Roberto's dilemma illustrates, emotional claustrophobia can arise not only from being faced with a set of choices, each of which is undesirable, but also from having relatively positive choices where every alternative holds advantages and none of the alternatives are disastrous.

Roberto finally saw the therapist, but even then, feelings of suffocation made it difficult for him to consider his situation logically. "Nothing or nobody can help," he sighed to the therapist.

His therapist replied: "The truth is, you can't deal with this decision right now because you're too afraid of being suffocated by it. But maybe we can look at what happens inside your mind and heart when you feel so smothered. Would you like to give it a try? Maybe we can start by looking at some of your beliefs. For example, you just stated one of your beliefs: that the situation is hopeless and nobody can help you. Can you think of anything else you're believing right now?"

Roberto was able to identify the following beliefs:

If I turn down the overseas job assignment, (1) I am a bad father and husband because I'm depriving my family of the money that will improve their lives; (2) I am a bad employee for not doing my duty toward my company; and (3) I'm a coward for giving in to family pressures to stay with them rather than doing what's best for me professionally.

But he also believed:

If take the assignment and go overseas, (1) I'm a bad father and husband for leaving my family alone for many months; (2) I'm a coward for not standing up to company pressures; (3) I'm a masochist for depriving myself emotionally and sexually.

"What else are you believing when you feel suffocated?" the therapist asked.

"Who cares what I think? Don't you care about how I'm feeling? I feel terrible! What about my guilt? I feel so guilty—and angry!"

"Let's go with that—with your guilt and anger. What do you believe about yourself, others, or the situation that is making you feel so guilty and angry?" the therapist asked.

Roberto had to think awhile, but finally replied:

I believe that unless I come up with a decision that makes everyone happy, including myself, I'm a failure. Because I can't come up with such a perfect and clear-cut decision, I feel guilty and angry. I also feel guilty and angry because I need to talk to a therapist. I believe that I should make this decision all by myself and that it's a sign of weakness to ask for help. Men are supposed to "tough it out" and figure out answers to these things by themselves, not with a therapist!

My guilt also comes from not being honest with my wife or my boss. But I strongly believe that I can't be totally open with either of them because if they knew my true feelings they would reject and ridicule me. If I told my wife a part of me wanted to take this overseas job because it was professionally challenging, she might feel rejected and hurt or she might accuse me of being selfish and putting my career ahead of the family. And if I tell my employer about not wanting to leave my family, he might think I'm henpecked or a Momma's boy, too wimpy to leave home, or not committed enough to the company. Then he might not consider me for promotion or other challenging assignments.

After examining his beliefs, Roberto quickly observed that he had put himself in a no-win situation. His beliefs that no matter what he decided about the job, he would be a bad father and husband and a coward were major contributors to his feelings of suffocation. One by one, Roberto and the therapist examined some of Roberto's other beliefs for accuracy and usefulness.

First, was it really true that being a man meant making important decisions all alone? Did this mean that generals and presidents who needed advisors were not manly or that male police officers who conferred with detectives, judges, and other court staff to solve a case were stupid weaklings?

Secondly, was it really true that he couldn't share openly with his wife? Was the problem that she could not possibly understand why an interesting assignment might be appealing to him, or that he did not know how to put his dilemma into words? What were the costs of not sharing his conflict with his wife? Was it possible she might be not only be accepting of his various feelings, but also be able to offer some help?

Even if she wasn't accepting, would it not be useful to know that and to be able to assess *how* upset she would be if he took the job overseas? For example, would she be slightly unhappy, very unhappy, or so unhappy she would threaten divorce? Would she be annoyed, somewhat angry, or furious? Was it possible that she might think the extra money was worth the separation?

Was the problem his wife's reaction or his belief that being a good husband meant he had to show 100 percent devotion to the family 100 percent of the time? If he believed that, where did that belief come from? Did he also believe that being a good worker meant giving 100 percent dedication to the job 100 percent of the time? If he believed that, where did that belief come from? In addition, did he believe he had to give his all to his family and his job at the same time? If so, where did he learn that belief?

Thirdly, a part of Roberto's fear of suffocation came from feeling as if his boss had given him an ultimatum: take this overseas assignment or put your job status at risk. His feelings of suffocation might lessen if there was some way he could exert some control over the situation. Simply talking to his boss would be a self-assertive act which, in itself, could help relieve Roberto's feelings of being ordered around. But Roberto's belief that he couldn't talk to his superiors stood in the way of such a dialogue.

The therapist asked Roberto to clarify this belief: Was it really true he could not talk with his superiors about the job assignment? What exactly was it he was afraid to say? What *could* he say or ask and still feel safe? Was it possible for Roberto to explore his degrees of freedom regarding this overseas assignment without making statements (such as that he was afraid of getting homesick) that could be held against him on the job? For example, could he ask if part of the work could be done at home; if the long assignment could be broken down into shorter segments, permitting him to return home for visits; or if he could be assigned to several short overseas projects rather than to one long one?

"At last, breathing room! Maybe I can talk to my wife and boss—a little," Roberto stated. After speaking with his wife, Roberto felt even less smothered because he no longer was carrying the guilt of harboring a secret from her. Furthermore, talking to her had given him the valuable information that she felt conflicted about what to do just like he did. Roberto was also able to speak to his employers about possible options. Even though they could not offer him any alternatives, the fact that he took the initiative to inquire about possible flexibility in the work schedule gave Roberto some sense of power and control in the situation, which further reduced his feelings of engulfment.

Roberto's decision was a hard one. Examining his beliefs did not make it crystal clear what he should do. However, by freeing himself of self-defeating, contradictory, and stifling beliefs (such as that he had to carry the burden alone and that no matter what he did, it would be the wrong decision), he was able to think about his decision more clearly, without being impeded by feelings of being smothered or stifled. Being able to talk to his wife, his employers, and other people made Roberto feel less isolated, guilty, and trapped, and therefore less angry, which virtually erased his feelings of suffocation.

Dora's Story

In contrast to Roberto, Dora's war within had negative origins. Dora observed that she felt smothered whenever she had to encounter her ex-husband at social or family events. If she had her choice, she would never see him again. But there were certain events, such as their children's school events and birthdays, that she felt obligated to attend for the sake of her children, even though it meant having to see him again.

It didn't matter how well she structured the event in order to avoid talking with him or sitting next to him at the table, or how much support she got for herself in the form of taking along a friend, within one hour of being in the same room with her ex-husband, she was overcome with emotional claustrophobia. Her greatest fear was losing control of herself and starting to curse or verbally abuse her former husband or beginning to overeat or consume too much alcohol in order to cope. Dora managed never lashed out at her ex-husband and she controlled her eating and drinking, but instead, she turned the stress inward, causing physical pain in her arms and legs.

To everyone else, Dora looked fine, but inside she feared she would be suffocated. A few times she wanted to curse at her ex-husband, but when she realized this would upset her children and other family members, her fantasy ceased. But her anxiety about having to encounter her ex-husband did not cease. In the future there would be not only more birthdays, but weddings, grandchildren, and other situations where, in order to participate in the event and be with her children, she would have to deal with his presence.

When Dora tried to put into words the beliefs she held while feeling suffocated by her ex-husband's presence, the only belief she could muster was, "Life is terrible because in order to be a good mother, I have to put up with seeing him again." With a little more effort, Dora realized that she believed, "The universe must hate me to torment me so and the reason I am tormented is because I am unworthy and destined for a life of misery because in my heart of hearts, I have not forgiven my ex for all of his wrongs."

Dora's therapist then asked her to consider if she might have a "war within"—a clash between two major emotional forces. Dora discovered that her "war within" was her love and loyalty to her children and her deep rage at her ex-husband for his abuse and betrayals. She was also angry at her children for not understanding her position and for not being willing to structure events so she and her ex-husband would not have to meet. Sometimes her children could accommodate her, for example, by having two Thanksgiving dinners, one with their father and one with their mother. But other events, such as graduations, religious ceremonies, and weddings, could not be duplicated to accommodate Dora's needs.

In examining her "war within," Dora came to realize that she was also angry at herself for not being as forgiving and tolerant as she wished she could be and as certain others in her life, especially her parents and children, wished she could be. She was also angry at her children for not totally rejecting their father the way she did. She wanted her children to cut themselves off from him and belong only to her. However, Dora knew that such an arrangement was not only emotionally impossible for her children, but also emotionally undesirable for them as well. Would she really want her children to not have a relationship with their father and for them to experience the bitterness and resentment she felt?

Dora was also able to identify four underlying beliefs: (1) I am a bad mother because I want my children to resent and dislike their father the way I do and to vindicate me by rejecting their father as I do. (2) I am admitting to my children and the world that my ex-husband was right and I was wrong by acting politely toward him in public. (3) I am a bad person because I cannot forgive my husband 100 percent the way others expect me to. (4) I deserve to have a bad time and to suffer emotional claustrophobia at these events as a punishment for having negative thoughts and feelings toward my ex-husband.

As a result of examining her beliefs, Dora realized that she was not a bad mother nor a morally deficient person because she still had negative feelings toward her ex-husband. She also realized that wishing that her children reject their father the way she did was a far cry from actually manipulating her children into such rejection and that behaving appropriately toward him at family functions was not an admission that her ex-husband was "right," but rather an attempt to support her children in their development.

She was further able to diffuse her emotional claustrophobia by realizing that the anger she experienced in anticipation of such events had many levels: not only was she angry at her ex-husband for his former mistreatment of her, but she also was angry at those people in her life who expected her to be a forgiving saint and at her children for not taking her side against their father. She was also angry at herself for having selfish and hostile thoughts, for expecting herself to be a model of spiritual perfection, and for still having part of her emotional energy bound up with her past relationship. By being able to uncover the complexity of her emotional reactions, she was better able to manage family events and not allow her past sorrows and angers to rob her of the joys available to her in the present.

Which of Your Beliefs Are Self-Defeating?

Have before you a list of the beliefs you held during each of the three incidents you are working on. You are now going to evaluate each belief by asking the following questions for each (write your evaluations of each belief in the second column, "Evaluation"):

1. How accurate is this belief?

> Be on guard for *all-or-nothing* beliefs and for *life-and-death* beliefs. Unless you are in immediate danger, such beliefs are probably untrue. Similarly, any belief that holds that you or another person will die as the result of something you do or say is probably also untrue, unless you are involved in a known life-threatening situation, such as domestic violence, war, or a criminal attack.

> For example, beliefs such as, "It will kill my _____, if I don't _____," or "There's nothing I can do about it," are untrue beliefs. Unless there is a direct causal relationship between your behavior and the injury or death of another, nothing you do will actually kill another. Similarly, unless you are being held captive or are very young, it's highly unlikely there is *nothing* you can do to help yourself or improve the situation.

> Exceptions are situations involving children or mentally or medically ill persons. In these situations, expressing how you feel openly and honestly may not "kill" the person, but may be severely detrimental, depending on the circumstances. Sensitivity is needed in dealing with persons who are severely ill and whose condition could be made worse by emotional shocks or stress. If you are dealing with fear of engulfment issues involving people who are psychologically or physically vulnerable or fragile, it is highly recommended that you consult with that individual's physician and discuss your plan of action with a qualified mental health professional.

Also, be on guard for beliefs that hold that you are worthless, incompetent, unlovable, undeserving, or inherently inferior. Such beliefs are not true and are extremely self-defeating and self-limiting. For example, Roberto's belief that no matter what he decided he would be a coward and a failure was untrue and counterproductive.

2. Does this belief help you think of loving creative ways of handling the situation, or does this belief immobilize you, make you furious or depressed, or make you want to isolate yourself from others?

3. Does this belief limit you? If so, how?

4. Think of someone you care about (a child, nephew, niece, or best friend), or think about someone you admire (a leader in your community or school). Imagine that this person held this belief. For each belief, would you want that individual to hold that belief? Would that belief help or limit that individual? Would that belief be accurate for that individual? If not, why not? If the belief is untrue for that individual, then why is true about you?

Desired Beliefs

In a separate page in your journal (one for each incident) entitled "Desired Beliefs" draw a line down the middle of the page. Label the left-hand column "What I Believe" and the right-hand column "Desired Beliefs." In the left-hand column, make a list of all the beliefs you've identified and decided are inaccurate and self-limiting.

For each belief you listed in the first column, ask "What do I want to believe?" or "What would I like to believe?" Write the desired belief in the second column.

For example, under "What I Believe," Roberto wrote, "Whatever decision I make about the job will be wrong because I will be betraying someone or something I care about" and "If either my boss or my wife is upset with my decision, this means I am a bad and inadequate person." Under "Desired Beliefs" he wrote, "I am a man who is deeply loyal to his family, his work, and himself."

Nick completed this exercise on his fear of engulfment that came up whenever his girlfriend pointed out that he had forgotten to complete some small chore he had promised to do for her. The following is from his Desired Beliefs chart:

Nick's Desired Beliefs

What I Believe	Desired Beliefs
When I forget to do something, it means I'm an inadequate male.	When I forget to do something, I'm just an average person who sometimes forgets.
When I forget to do something, my girlfriend will think I'm an inadequate male.	My girlfriend doesn't get upset about these small things. It's okay for her to remind me.

As Nick completed this exercise, he realized another underlying belief was, "If I don't please my girlfriend, she'll yell at me and leave me." Upon examining this belief, Nick discovered that this belief was appropriate for his relationship with his ex-wife, not his girlfriend. In his marriage, he had felt engulfed because he was trapped between wanting to be a loyal family man and needing to end a relationship where he was being financially and emotionally exploited. His new girlfriend was not like his ex-wife and had no financial power over him. Also, unlike his wife who often yelled at him, his girlfriend hardly raised her voice at anyone.

After completing this exercise, whenever Nick's girlfriend pointed out his failure to complete certain chores, Nick would still start to experience emotional claustrophobia. But he was able to stop the fear from growing by checking his beliefs. "What am I believing now?" he'd ask himself. "I'm believing that if someone points out a small mistake I made, I'm going to be yelled at and abandoned. But I know that this isn't true anymore. It used to be true, but it isn't true now. Making a mistake now won't mean any of that, so there's nothing to be afraid of."

Part II

Identifying
Self-Defeating Beliefs

Chapter 7

Making a Plan

In this chapter, you will be making a plan on how to handle the fear of engulfment incidents you have been working on. Like the captain of a boat, you will determine the direction of your ship, map the emotional territory you will be traveling, and plan for handling the predictable and unpredictable emotional storms that almost always accompany situations and people who cause you to experience emotional claustrophobia.

Why You Need a Plan

Trying to manage your fear of engulfment is like sailing on uncharted waters. You may have a destination in mind or perhaps you are simply trying to enjoy the ride. Whether or not you have a particular goal in mind, you are certain of one thing: you no longer want the winds and seas to toss you around and strike terror in your heart. You also don't want to be trapped on a boat you cannot guide or command. You want to determine your own direction or, at the very least, feel safe in the direction you're heading.

In real life, your adversaries are not the forces of nature, but instead your foes are your emotional reactions to other human beings and difficult situations. In the past, you may have felt you were no match for these powerful people or overwhelming situations, causing you to give them authority over you. As a result, you likely felt helpless, hopeless, and without any defenses.

You may be no match for a hurricane or unruly seas, but in the world of human events and human relations, you have some power, at the very least the power to state what you want and need. The situation may be overpowering and the others involved have power also. Perhaps they have an emotional hold over you. But unless you are being held captive in a life-threatening situation, you are not entirely powerless. You probably have more power than you think. You just don't know how to use it. Also, unlike being alone on a small ship in unruly waters, you don't have to weather the storm alone. You can ask others to be your emotional life raft: to offer support when you're in need, whether they're standing by your side or willing to be available by phone or e-mail.

If you plan to take some action in the unruly seas of human relationships or difficult situations, and you're ready to try to minimize (or at least manage) that horrible fear of being smothered, you will need a plan. As John Steinbeck wrote in his novel *The Pearl*, "A plan is a real thing." This plan should include a "map" and emergency provisions, in case you make a wrong turn or the opposing forces manage to temporarily overwhelm you.

You can plan your journey carefully in every detail, and you try to avoid known hazardous areas, such as whirlpools and shark-infested waters. However, you also need to expect the unexpected and prepare for it as best you can.

You should also expect those moments, and there may be many of them, where you want to give up the journey and just turn around and go back to where you started. Change, even positive change, can be excruciatingly painful and just as frightening as the fear of being smothered. There will be times when the prospect of being free of feeling smothered won't seem liberating and exciting, it will feel dangerous.

Unlike your fear of engulfment, with which you're all too familiar, what lies ahead has yet to be defined. You don't know how your relationships, your self-identity, or your life situations might unfold when you are free of feeling smothered. Anita, who had already made major strides toward overcoming her fear of engulfment, found that at various points in time "it was scary to be so free. I wondered if I'd rather feel suffocated and oppressed by someone rather than have all of those new choices."

From where will you find the courage to leave what was safe and secure, your old place of fear of engulfment, and open yourself to new possibilities? Perhaps you can find some inspiration in that, according to Joseph Campbell in *The Power of Myth* (1988), true heroes and heroines are people who must leave their homeland and embark into unknown territory. Often they must contend with enemies, including humans, animals, monsters, supernatural beings, and their own limitations as human beings. But they have a goal, a mission, something precious they are trying to find or save, and for that goal they are willing to endure the hardships and fight whatever battles need to be fought.

If you seek to overcome some of your emotional claustrophobia, then you are a hero or heroine, too. The precious entity you are trying to find or save is your sense of having some control over your life, as well as your freedom to interact or engage in as many situations as possible without being filled with dread that you'll feel suffocated.

At the end of myths, heroes and heroines always return home from their adventures with a gift—a treasure of some kind, whether it be increased wealth or wisdom or something of spiritual significance. If you pursue the hero or heroine's course and do not forsake the mission, even when it seems appealing to return home, then eventually you will return home, and you will have a gift to give as well.

At the very least, you will have more of yourself to give to others and various situations. The energy that was absorbed by feeling engulfed, anticipating being engulfed, recuperating from feeling smothered, and planning how you would endure people or situations that caused you to feel suffocated will be available to use for other purposes and to share with those people and activities that you cherish.

If you have completed the written exercises thus far, you already have a map of the emotional field you are traveling in. (In fact, you have three maps, one for each emotionally claustrophobic incident you have been working on.) These maps describe the situations and people involved and the way you interact with them, as well as your thoughts, feelings, and beliefs. But these maps are incomplete.

Missing from these maps are indications of your destination, of where would like to go. Also, you need more equipment. If you have practiced some of the calming exercises in chapter 5, you already have some important tools. If you completed the exercises in chapter 6, you have available to you new more desirable beliefs, which can help you be more expressive and assertive in situations that used to silence or paralyze you.

Having Realistic Hopes

All change, even desired change, is difficult. Learning new ways of reacting and thinking is also difficult and takes time and practice. Do not expect yourself to be totally transformed as the result of reading this book and working on its exercises. And do not be surprised if, despite your efforts, your old self-defeating beliefs have not disappeared. Suppose you have spent decades believing that refusing the requests of relatives is a sign of disloyalty to the family, and that this belief is held by most of the people who shaped your life and who are emotionally important to you. Under such circumstances, would it be realistic for you to expect this belief to totally vanish or to be quickly or easily replaced by the new, more desirable belief that it is okay to refuse some family requests?

Old beliefs die hard. However, as the result of your efforts, you now have new beliefs available to you and you will be increasingly able to act on these new beliefs, rather than the old self-defeating ones, if you choose to.

Similarly, you should not expect yourself to be totally calm as the result of practicing breathing, muscle relaxation, or other self-calming exercises. If you suffer from fear of engulfment, you may never be completely cool, calm, and collected as you enter situations that trigger this fear. A part of you may always be afraid, anxious, insecure, and/or unhappy with certain people or in particular situations. To be totally calm in a situation fraught with emotionally claustrophobic memories would be difficult for anyone! The goal is not to be totally serene, but to be able to reduce your anxiety and tension sufficiently so as to stop the vicious cycle where your fears of being smothered or stifled create even greater feelings of suffocation.

How to Make a Plan

Making a plan requires several steps. In this chapter, you will add to the information you already have about your emotional claustrophobia and make a solid plan for managing your fear of engulfment in the present. The first step involves visualizing the three fear of engulfment incidents you have been working on; the second, identifying your goals for each situation; and the third, identifying critical choice points, times during these incidents where you had real choices. You will then need to develop and strengthen a mind-set that is based on beliefs that are functional rather than self-defeating and immobilizing. You will also need to master certain communication skills, such as "I" messages.

Once you have completed all of this groundwork, you will be asked to visualize the problematic situation again—only this time you will imagine a desirable ending, rather than the usual ending that includes fears of engulfment. Also important is an emergency plan, a set of actions that can help minimize your fear of engulfment if your plan does not unfold as you anticipated.

The following exercises will help you make a plan for handling the three incidents of fear of engulfment on which you have been so diligently working. Complete each exercise for all three separate incidents.

Visualization Exercise

Find a comfortable and quiet place to sit and take three or four minutes to calm yourself using any self-calming method that works for you. Scan your body for tension in specific muscles. Relax those muscles as much as you can. Then turn to the section of your journal where you described a situation or person who usually leads to your emotional claustrophobia. Conjure up a picture of the specific person, situation, or incident in your mind's eye.

Visualize it as vividly as possible, putting in all colors, sounds, and smells you can remember. Then picture the incident as if you are watching it on a small-screened television or watching it as you are passing by on a train. You will still be able to see the incident clearly, but you will be less distracted by fear or by any wounding emotions that are part of the experience.

Another way of visualizing the incident is to form a picture of the incident in your mind and put it in a picture frame. Put in as many sensory details as you can remember, and then shrink the picture down until you can visualize holding it in your hands and hanging it on the wall.

If you are having problems with this exercise, try to visualize the situation, substituting another person in your place. The person needs to be someone you care about and wish to protect, not someone you dislike or disrespect.

After you have visualized the experience, write it down in your journal on a fresh page in your journal and title it "Visualization Experience—Incident #1."

After you complete the visualization experience for the other two incidents you have been working on, write about them in your journal in pages labeled "Visualization Experience—Incident #2" and "Visualization Experience—Incident #3."

Annette visualized the following incident:

> *I go home for the Fourth of July weekend and within the first fifteen minutes, Mom asks me to go swimming.*
> *   I'm furious! My mom knows I've been in therapy about the symbiotic relationship we used to have. I've told her a dozen times*

that I can't do things that remind me of being so close to her, like swimming, where she'd tell me all her secrets and say how special I was and how she couldn't live without me, etc., etc. The last thing in the world I want to do is go swimming with her. But with all the rest of the family around, I don't want to make a scene. So I tell my mom I'm tired.

Then my mother insists. "Why don't you want to go? We used to go together all the time when you were a little girl. If you're tired, you don't have to swim. Just go along and keep me company."

I look at her, hoping my eyes don't show my anger. I'm afraid to talk, lest I say something nasty. My mom comes toward me as if she's going to pat my hand and I feel myself being engulfed, as if I'm becoming joined to her. I shut down emotionally. I can move my body, but my feelings are frozen.

My mom keeps insisting that I go swimming and I'm turning more and more into a robot. When I try to speak, I start feeling smothered again and all that comes out of me is a squeak.

I'm frantic for a way out. All I can think of is to promise my mother I'll go swimming with her the next day. But she doesn't buy it. She starts crying and talking about how I don't love her anymore. My dad stares at me like I'm a witch.

I know when I'm licked, so I agree to go swimming. In the car on the way to the pool, my mom talks like everything is just fine, but I feel absolutely smothered. I feel like a nonhuman. Even the cold water doesn't make me feel alive. When my mom tries to make conversation in the pool, I ignore her, afraid that if I start to talk, I'll tell her how much I detest her constant need of me and that I'll never come visit again unless she leaves me alone. Deep down, I wonder why I torture myself trying to have a relationship with her at all, but the thought of kicking my mother out of my life seems terrifying and morally unacceptable.

The more my mom talks, the more I avoid her or answer with one-syllable replies like, "yes." "no," "that's nice," or "I don't know." By this time I feel like dying, but I play the part. My mom asks me what is wrong and I tell her that I think I'm getting the flu. My mom gets upset. We get out of the pool and go home.

Identifying Your Goals

Review your visualization experience and ask yourself, "What was my goal in the situation? What was I trying to achieve? What did I want?" Write a few sentences about your goals in the situation. State your goals in terms of your behavior and actions, not the actions or feelings of others.

For example, suppose Annette wrote, "My goal is to have my mother apologize for all the harm she did to me," or "My goal is to have my mother (or other family members) understand why I have to put limits on my contact with my mother." These may be legitimate desires; however, Annette cannot control her mother or family. She can only control her own actions. Hence she must state her goals in terms of what she will or will not do.

Rethinking her goals from this perspective, Annette wrote:

> *I want to talk with my mother, but not in situations like swimming and not about subjects like sports, which remind me of my past overinvolvement with her. My goal is to not automatically go along with whatever my mom wants, which is what I've always done. I want to think about what's right and good for me, not just her. If my mom wants to go swimming and I don't, I will refuse the request and not be coerced into it. If she wants to talk about subjects that are a problem for me, I will tell her that I do not wish to discuss these subjects at this time and suggest ones I would like to discuss instead.*

Identifying Critical Choice Points

Reflect back on your visualization and read your journal entry on this experience. As you go over what happened, pay close attention to any points during the incident where you (or whomever you've substituted for yourself) felt you had a choice or where you acted on a choice. On a fresh page in your journal entitled "Choice Points" answer the following questions (for each incident):

What choices do you see were available? Were you aware of these choices during the time you were having the experience? Which choices were you aware of at the time and which choices have you become aware of as a result of working on these exercises?

Looking back, do you wish you had acted differently? If so, how? What choices would you have made at the available choice points if you were holding to your desired beliefs, as opposed to your old beliefs?

For each situation, write five or six sentences about how you wish you could have managed the situation paying particular attention to actions you could have taken (or not taken) during critical choice points.

Of the choices you were aware of at the time, on which choices did you act? How did you feel as you decided to act on these choices? What beliefs or thoughts were you having when you made the decision to act? (Refer to your journal entries regarding your beliefs, from chapter 6, to help you answer this question.)

Of the choices you were aware of at the time, which choices did you decide *not* to take action on? What were your thoughts as you decided *not* to act on these choices?

Did there come a point in time during the incident where you felt you had *no* choices. What beliefs did you have at that time? What choices do you wish had been available to you?

At this point, check to be sure that you are still relaxed. If you need to practice one of your breathing or relaxation exercises at this time, do so.

Some of the critical choice points Annette identified were:

1. I could have refused to go swimming from the very beginning by just saying no repeatedly or by coming up with a more dramatic excuse, like saying that I had a rash that couldn't get wet.

2. Instead of discussing the issue in front of the whole family, which put pressure on me to be a "good girl," I could have asked to speak to my mother alone. Being alone with her scares me, but being outnumbered is even scarier.

3. I could have reminded her of my issues with being physically close to her and her agreement to respect my boundaries about swimming and other such activities.

4. I could have asked other family members to come along, thus diluting my mother's impact.

5. I could have taken charge of the conversation in the pool, asking my mother questions I was interested in rather than let her dominate the conversation, just like she did all during my growing years.

6. I could have driven my own car or taken enough money for a taxi so I could leave any time I wanted, or I could have called a friend to pick me up.

7. At any point in time, I could have told my mother some of my feelings. It wouldn't have changed my mother, but it would have made me feel better.

At the time Annette felt that the only choices she had were to go along with her mother, to distance herself from her mother by withdrawing and limiting the conversation, or to use lies as a means of escape.

The one choice Annette *did* act on was lying to her mother. Lying caused Annette some guilt, but Annette felt that guilt was a small price to pay for the enormous sense of relief she felt at having some way to ward off the fear of engulfment stimulated by her mother's demands. Once she got in her mother's car and went to the pool, she felt completely powerless and without choices.

When Annette was asked to write down the beliefs she held when she failed to act on her choices, she listed the following beliefs: "I am not allowed to talk back to my mother. I have to say yes to my mother if she cries or looks upset. I have to do what my mother wants. Only horrible ungrateful children tell their parents they are angry or upset with them just because the parents want to spend time with them. If I speak up, my mother will be so hurt and angry she'll never talk to me again. I can't control my anger so I better not say anything. I don't deserve to be angry, my mother wasn't so bad to me even if she was symbiotic."

The beliefs she would like to have included: "I can control my anger. I can love my mother and still say no to her. It's okay to disagree with my mother. I've worked hard in therapy to establish boundaries. It's not okay for my mother to violate them."

Updating Your Beliefs: Old and New

Refer back to your list from chapter 6, where you listed the beliefs you held during a fear of engulfment episode. Now examine your responses in the Choice Points exercise you just completed. Are there any beliefs you want to add to this list?

In a similar manner, refer back to your list of desired beliefs from chapter 6. Now review the beliefs you held that enabled you to take positive action during any choice points that were available. Do any of these need to be added to your Desired Beliefs list?

Keep these desired beliefs in mind as you answer the following questions in your journal: Looking back, do you wish you had acted differently? If so, how? Which choices would you have made at the available choice points if you were holding your desired beliefs, as opposed to your old beliefs?

For each situation, write five or six sentences about how you wish you could have managed the situation, paying particular attention to actions you could have taken (or not taken) during critical choice points.

The Right Mind-Set

"But Kino had lost his old world and he must clamber on to a new one. For his dream of the future was real and never to be destroyed, and he had said, 'I will go,' and that made a real thing too. To determine to go and to say it is to be half way there," wrote John Steinbeck in his novel *The Pearl* (53). Kino puts into words his determination not to be cheated out of the good things in life. Like Kino, it is important that you determine to overcome your fear of engulfment and speak the words that will help you reach that goal.

You have put both your old beliefs and your desired beliefs, into words. Now you are going to be asked to say them aloud. Speaking them will make them more real for you. You will see more clearly how self-defeating and psychologically unhealthy some of your old beliefs are. Speaking your desired beliefs will also help to implant them more firmly in your memory.

This exercise requires you to read aloud (to yourself, or to a friend or therapist if you choose) the list of beliefs you held that prevented you from taking positive action on your own behalf at any choice points. How did it feel to state these beliefs aloud? In your journal on a fresh piece of paper entitled "How My Old Beliefs Harm Me," write five or six sentences about how these beliefs emotionally harm you and hold back your growth.

The second part of this exercise requires you to read aloud your list of *desired* beliefs. How did it feel to state these beliefs aloud? In your journal on a fresh piece of paper entitled "My Desired Beliefs," write five or six sentences about how these desired beliefs can help you and what it feels like to allow yourself to hold beliefs that work *for* you rather than *against* you.

Communication Skills

In previous exercises, you identified some of your goals and worked on evaluating self-defeating beliefs and replacing them with more self-loving ones. You will soon be asked to visualize your three fear of engulfment situations in terms of how you would like them to occur. Yet before you visualize your desired outcome, you need to be aware of and utilize certain communication skills in order to be effective.

The Need for Communication Skills

Glance over the following section and if the suggestions are familiar to you and you are comfortable communicating in these ways, then skip this section and go on to the next chapter. However, be certain of your mastery of these communication skills and your ability to use them in a situation that feels emotionally claustrophobic. Even if you have good communication skills, it may be worth the extra time and effort to complete the written exercises in this section, because under the stress of a fear of engulfment, your usual abilities to communicate may be diminished by your anxiety.

Setting Boundaries

If a certain person creates a fear of engulfment in you and you do not have to or do not want to have a relationship with that person, you really don't have a problem. All you have to do is avoid that person and never see him or her again—if you can help it. However, choosing not to have a relationship with a person who makes you afraid of being smothered may not be an option for you. You may want to have a relationship with that person, you may be working with that individual, or you may be forced to encounter that person because he or she is part of your family. The dilemma of such situations is wanting or needing to have a positive, working, or at least cordial relationship with that individual without feeling so trapped by him or her. In personal or intimate relationships, you may want more than the absence of emotional claustrophobia: you may want a more mature, authentic relationship with a particular individual, without the accompanying fear of engulfment.

The solution to this dilemma involves setting boundaries or limits on what you will or won't do in your relationship. This requires that you know your wishes, limits, and needs. However, it is not enough for *you* to know your needs and limitations. You must able to communicate these to the other person involved in a manner that is respectful of both yourself and the other individual. For this, you will need to acquire and practice certain communication skills. Insisting on your boundaries in a hostile, abusive, or accusatory manner may get you the space you need, but you may also lose the relationship.

Suppose you are trying to set limits with family members, close friends, and other special intimates. If your means of communication is personally attacking or denigrating, the other person may retaliate in kind or disintegrate into tears, sadness, or pain. At this point, you may be sorely tempted to retract your boundaries.

For example, Marie's mother-in-law was always insisting that Marie sample her cookies. Marie did not want the cookies. On one occasion, Marie's mother-in-law literally put cookies on Marie's plate. Marie lashed out. "Take those terrible tasting cookies off my plate. And stop interfering with my eating! Are you going to start interfering with my marriage next? If you don't stop being so intrusive, I won't let you visit your grandchildren!"

Marie was following the suggestion given to her by others to be "completely open" with her anger. Fighting and being completely expressive of anger are methods that some therapists and self-help books recommend. However, the idea that open expression of anger is always helpful simply isn't the case: the usefulness of such open sharing depends on the individual's goal.

If Marie's objective was simply to speak her mind and she did not care about having a long-term friendly relationship with her mother-in-law, her communication was consistent with her goal. However, if her goal was to establish boundaries in an ongoing relationship with her mother-in-law, then raging at her mother-in-law, criticizing her cookies, and making threats about the future would be counterproductive.

In situations where you have an emotional bond with the other person and you value that bond, any hurt you create by being attacking might cause you so much guilt that you retract your boundaries. For example, if Marie's mother-in-law had begun to weep or if other family members had chastised Marie for being so angry, Marie might have felt so guilty that she would have retracted her statements and eaten the cookies.

In *The Dance of Anger*, Harriet Lerner (1985) describes how open expressions of anger about being intruded upon or engulfed can sometimes serve to perpetuate the problem rather than solve it. She suggests that simply stating your needs and wishes is more respectful of yourself and the other person, and ultimately, this route is more effective in establishing boundaries than a yelling match of mutual accusations.

For instance, Marie's goal was to set a boundary in her relationship with her mother-in-law. However, Marie's lashing out only led to subsequent guilt and family pressures, which only served to put Marie under further domination by her mother-in-law. Marie would have been far more effective if she had spoken to her mother-in-law in a calm but firm manner: "I know how much time and love you put into making those cookies and I can appreciate why you want me to have some of them. But I really don't want any cookies right now and I like to put food on my own plate and not have others do that for me." In this manner, Marie would have communicated her needs and wants without denigrating or blaming her mother-in-law.

"I" Messages

A basic communication skill is the "I" message, which is to be contrasted with the "you" message. An "I" message is a statement about how you feel or think or about what you want or need. In contrast, a "you" message is accusatory—it blames another person or situation for how you feel. "I feel uncomfortable reviewing the same information three times" is an "I" message. "This is a useless meeting. You're wasting my time," is a "you" message.

Saying, "You're greedy," is not an "I" message. If someone is being greedy, an I-message response would be, "When you want most of the money for yourself, I am afraid that I won't have enough for me." If someone is driving over the speed limit, instead of saying, "You're driving dangerously," you can communicate your feelings and the actions you plan to take as a result of your feelings by saying, "I'm uncomfortable when you drive this fast. If you insist on driving over the speed limit, I will need to find another way home."

"I" messages are not criticisms of yourself, but neither are they criticisms of others. When you give "I" messages, you are telling someone what you will or will not do and how you feel. You are taking responsibility for your thoughts, feelings, and needs. Even though you may feel the other person is wrong and doesn't have the right to feel the way they do, it's important to focus on what you want or need from the situation. There is nothing wrong with wanting certain people to change their views, feelings, or behaviors. But the reality is that it is very hard to change others or to try to convince them that your position is the correct one. As Lerner (1985) points out in *The Dance of Anger*, maturity involves acknowledging the reality of multiple realities and understanding that people think, feel, and react differently.

Your anger at others for being the way they are may be completely legitimate and may present a problem for you. But two even greater problems are not knowing what you need or want in the situation, and not acting on what you know is true about yourself in order to stay connected to the other person. Your best bet is to focus on how you want to relate or stay connected to that person, communicating your thoughts, feelings, or limitations as best as you can. If the individual is abusive, it is also important to protect yourself and make yourself safe.

Consider the example of Annette, who experienced fear of engulfment when she was physically close to her mother. Annette could have made blaming accusatory statements, such as, "It's your fault I don't want to spend time with you. You ruined my childhood and made me neurotic," or "There you go—being dependent on me again. When are you going to grow up?" Annette's observations about her mother's destructive impact on her life and her mother's excessive dependency on her are not imaginary: they are psychologically accurate. However, her mother undoubtedly would perceive Annette's comments as attacks and respond either with hurt or anger. Because the comments were negative and were stated in anger, Annette might feel guilty and then apologize or retract her comments.

But if Annette used "I" messages, she could escape any guilt inherent in denigrating or arguing with another. Simply stating one's feelings and needs is not an attack and is not a cause for guilt. For example, Annette could have said: "I don't want to go swimming," or "I'd like to do something with you, like _____ , but I do not wish to go swimming with you," or "Mother, swimming isn't good for me (makes me uncomfortable) right now. Maybe in the future we can go swimming togther, but right now it's best for me to do something like _____ ." Annette's mother could still respond with hurt and anger and, observing her mother's reaction, Annette could still feel guilty, but Annette's guilt would not be based on having verbally attacked or demeaned her mother.

"I" messages are hardest to think of and to say when you're angry. If you're anticipating a situation where you fear being engulfed, especially if you anticipate being angry, you may want to prepare your communications in advance and practice them aloud or with a friend. In this way, you will be better able to express yourself at a time when your verbal and other mental abilities are not at their best due to anxiety and anger.

For example, Daniel felt smothered by his stepfather's comments on his muscular build. Ever since Daniel had become an adolescent, his stepfather had openly expressed jealousy of Dan's vitality and physical strength. Daniel had asked his stepfather to stop making such comments, but he was unable, or chose not to, respect Dan's wishes:

> *I've decided it's unconscious. I can't tell my stepdad he's acting jealous of me and to please stop it, because when I've tried to bring the subject up, he can't understand what I'm talking about. He either switches the subject or acts like I'm overreacting or making things up. No matter what I say to him, he stays in denial over his jealousy, even though it's colored my entire childhood. I've even tried making jokes out of his comments or limiting my time talking with him. But no matter how short my conversations with him are, he always finds a way to make some comment about my build. Then I feel all guilty and angry—engulfed.*
>
> *I found myself wishing the whole problem would go away—but that's not going to happen. So I decided that whenever he makes a jealous comment, I'd either use an "I" message like, "I feel unhappy when you talk about my body," or just change the subject by asking him something about his life or something else that matters to him.*

Maintaining Eye Contact

When you are expressing yourself, it is important to maintain eye contact with the other person. If you are having an important communication, it's important to set the stage by interacting in a place free of distractions and interruptions.

The Broken-Record Technique

If the other person is insisting on a point or he or she wishes to engage you in an argument by attacking you, you can use the broken record technique of repeating your statement of your needs and limitations. For example, if Marie's mother-in-law continues to insist on giving Marie cookies, Marie can simply repeat, "I don't want any cookies right now. Thank you." Similarly, if Daniel's stepfather goes on a tirade about Daniel being delusional or overly sensitive, Daniel can simply repeat, "I feel unhappy when you talk about my body." In expressing your wants and your uncomfortable feelings, you are taking a risk, but it is a positive one.

People can argue with you about your opinions and beliefs, but they can't legitimately argue about your feelings. Your feelings just are. Of course, there will be people who will tell you that you "shouldn't feel that way" or imply that you don't "have the right to feel that way." Your reply could be, "This is the way I feel. Maybe I shouldn't feel this way or maybe I should. You may not feel the same way as I do in this situation, but this is how I feel, for whatever reason."

Connected but Free: Maintaining Connection without Engulfment

Last, but not least, if you are the one who is setting the boundary and you also want to have an ongoing relationship with that individual, it is up to you to try to maintain the connection. It is your responsibility to state to the other individuals any sincere, positive feelings you have about them and what you do value about your relationship with them. You can also show empathy for their position by saying, "I can appreciate how you feel." Then, without attacking their feelings or behavior, you can state your needs or limitations.

The positive statements you make need to be sincere. Telling a person that they matter to you and that you understand why they feel the way they do is a valid and effective communication only if it is true and comes from your heart. Otherwise, making positive and caring statements are forms of manipulation. Part of the power of your communication lies in your honesty. If you are lying or fabricating half-truths in order to get your way or minimize the anger or rejection you anticipate receiving as the result of taking a stand, then your communication will be not only unethical, but also weak. The communication techniques suggested in this chapter are not intended to be used to deceive others, but instead to contribute to the building of an emotionally mature and honest relationship.

For example, Annette could tell her mother, "Mom, I can appreciate why you want to go swimming with me. You miss me and miss the times when all your children were home with you. If I were in your shoes, I'd want to do something with my daughter, too. But I don't want to go swimming. It's important for me to not go, but to do something else instead." Marie could say, "I can understand why you want me to have your cookies. You are very proud of your baking and I'm sure the cookies are absolutely delicious. But I don't want any cookies right now."

If you can find just *one* positive aspect of the other person's communication or *one* aspect of the other person's position with which you can empathize, state that to the other person. Then let them know your needs and limits. You don't have to justify your needs or limitations. All you have to do is state them clearly and unambiguously, without attacking the other person. If you are criticized, instead of becoming defensive or attacking, you could show some empathy in a reply such as, "I can appreciate your feelings" or "I can see why you might feel that way."

Recommended guides to assertive communication techniques are listed in the appendix.

Your Desired Outcome

In this exercise, you are going to be asked to suspend your belief and imagine what might seem impossible: that you will no longer experience emotional claustrophobia in the situations where, in the past, having this fear was almost inevitable. Before you begin this exercise, read your desired beliefs aloud one more time, review your journal entry about what it is like to be able to have supportive beliefs, and review the basic communication skills principles of "I" messages, maintaining eye contact, and affirming the positive aspects of the other person and your relationship with that person.

Then, as you did in the previous visualization exercise, find a comfortable place to sit, close your eyes, and use your breathing or muscle relaxation exercises (or whatever method you have of calming yourself) to relax. If you use physical exercise to calm yourself, then plan to complete your second visualization after you exercise. At all times, scan your body for tension and try to relax those areas that are still tense.

Then imagine the incident where you experienced emotional claustrophobia. Fantasize the most favorable sequence of events. What would be the best ending to this incident? What would it take to make the fantasy a reality? What limits would you need to set on others? What actions could you take to protect yourself, stand up for yourself, or manage your reactions?

As you visualize this desirable outcome, keep in mind your goals for the situation, your desired beliefs, and the suggested communication skills, such as "I" messages. If you have difficulties imagining a desirable outcome, then substitute another person for yourself, someone whom you cherish and respect.

On a fresh page in your journal entitled "My Desired Outcome—Incident #1" write seven or eight sentences about your desired outcome. Take some time to do some deep breathing, muscle relaxation, or other self-calming exercises. Review what you have written and ask yourself the following questions: Have I tried to meet my goals? Were my actions guided by my desired beliefs, rather than my old self-defeating beliefs? Did I try to use the communication skills described in this chapter? Then, if you need to, revise your description of your desired outcome to include a closer approximation of your goals, a closer adherence to your desired beliefs, and improved communication skills.

Annette wrote:

> *My goal is to be able to go home so I can feel like I have a family, but not be forced to do things that remind me of the negative parts of my past in that home. My old belief was that I couldn't say no. My new belief is that I'm entitled to set limits. My fantasy is that I'll refuse my mother's request to go swimming and that she will accept it without crying or accusing me of not loving her. But that will never happen. So my next fantasy is that I say no to my mother's request to go swimming and not change my mind, even if she starts crying or my dad starts giving me dirty looks. I ask to speak to my mom privately, deciding within myself not to bring up past psychological issues that my mother doesn't understand and that only threaten her and make her more emotional and clingy.*
>
> *Once alone with my mom, I look at her straight in the eyes and tell her I care about her, which is why I'm visiting her. Without bringing up the past, I simply tell her I don't want to go swimming but would enjoy doing something else with her, such as going for a walk or having lunch together.*

Emergency Plans

Exits

You need to have at least one exit planned. Plan several exits if you can. Having an exit plan isn't the same as avoiding, escaping, or being a coward. Be prepared with money, a vehicle, the phone number of friends who can help you in case you need to leave, and/or with plausible, emotionally neutral and nonprovocative reasons for taking a break or ending the interaction. Statements such as, "I need to take a break," "I need to leave now," "I'm not feeling well," or "I want to discuss this issue at a later time," are all means of breaking away that do not involve lying, attacking others, or being defensive.

If you have a supportive friend to call, you can say, "I need to make a phone call," and excuse yourself and call your friend. In especially difficult situations when friends are not available, you can leave messages on their answering service or even call your own answering service and give yourself an affirming message, such as, "I can survive this," "I deserve peace of mind," or "I'm not a horrible person because I need to set limits."

If you feel like leaving, but it is in your best interest not to and you decide that you need to stay a little longer, consider making a deal with yourself: you will *try* to stay for another limited period of time, for example, another fifteen minutes, and then reevaluate whether you need to leave or if you can stay a little longer. Keep negotiating with yourself for small bits of additional time, but always give yourself permission to try to leave the situation if you become too uncomfortable (or afraid, angry, entrapped, or engulfed).

For example, Keith experienced fear of engulfment at parties, brunches, and other social events, and after about an hour at any of these types of functions he would want to leave. But he felt he couldn't leave early without insulting his host or bringing attention to himself. Also, sometimes he had gotten a ride with others to the event and hesitated to ask them to leave early on his behalf. Because of all these factors, Keith had decided it was best for all concerned, himself and others, for him to not attend social gatherings.

As part of his efforts to manage his fear of engulfment, Keith needed to learn that there was no rule that if he accepted an invitation that he had to stay for all or most of the event. It was permissible to stay for a limited but comfortable period of time and then leave. He could ease matters by simply informing his hosts ahead of time of time that he might have to leave early. In addition, it was imperative that he allow himself to leave when he began to feel engulfed and that he have the means to leave. This meant that he had to drive to the event himself or, if he rode with others, have enough taxi money or some other means of getting home.

Keith decided to stay at one particular function for about an hour. After that hour, he could evaluate how he was feeling and if he needed to, he could leave as planned. But if he was enjoying himself, he could decide to stay another twenty minutes. After twenty minutes had passed and he still felt safe, he could reconsider his decision to leave once more. By negotiating with himself at various points along the way and by knowing that he could leave at any time, Keith was able to extend his attendance at social events long past his usual hour and a half.

Quick Fixes.

Here are a few suggestions for situations where you are in a public place or social situation and you need a breather (McKay et al. 1989):

- Spend ten seconds rubbing a tense part of your body.
- Take ten slow, deep breaths.
- Change your posture and stretch.
- Talk more slowly.
- Get up and get a cold (nonalcoholic) drink.
- Sit down and lean back.
- Blink your eyes and imagine your safe place.

Anticipating the Worst

You have a plan. But there are several more important questions to consider: What is the worst thing that can happen? Is there any way to predict the probability that the worst thing will happen? On the basis of past experiences and the information you have, what is the probability of the worst thing occurring? Should the worst outcome occur, what will you do?

Should the worst outcome occur, can you handle it?

All these questions need careful consideration. You will not be able to proceed on your plan for managing your fear of engulfment if, in doing so, you are impeded by the gnawing fear of "What if _____ happens." Any fears you have about the possible outcome of your plan must be identified and confronted. You must then assess how realistic your fears are. At this point, you may want to share your fears with your therapist or a trusted friend. These people may be able to help you sort your realistic fears from your unrealistic fears.

If following your plan might unleash the potential for harm to yourself or others, your plan needs to be put on hold or modified so that the possibility of physical injury is not an issue. Furthermore, if you feel that on a psychological level you could not handle a worst-case scenario, and you think that scenario is actually feasible, then you may need to modify your plan or postpone trying to implement it.

However, if you realize that the worst thing that can happen isn't that bad, then when you start to panic about implementing your plan, you can ask yourself, "What's the worst thing that can happen?" and you can assure yourself, "If the worst happens, nobody gets hurt and I can handle it."

Chapter 8

Living Your Plan

If you completed the exercises in chapter 7, you should now have a plan of action for three different fear of engulfment situations. Now you have a choice: either you can actively seek out one of these situations to try out one of your plans or you can wait until one of these situations presents itself and then use your plan.

Some people experience a sense of mastery and control by seeking out an opportunity to try out one of their plans, whereas others prefer to wait until the problem situation comes to them. Still others decide not to use any of their plans, even when confronted with a fear of engulfment situation they cannot avoid. The thought of changing their usual patterns of interacting seems too risky and dangerous.

There is no right or wrong decision in this matter. Seeking out a chance to try your new techniques or deciding to wait until you are forced to do so are both fine alternatives. Neither is there any shame in not feeling ready to use one of your plans. Perhaps you need more time to make the emotional adjustment of acting and thinking in new ways or perhaps your plan needs more work. You may need more time to think about or work on your plan or you may need more support from others.

Although it is important to challenge yourself and to not let your fear of engulfment control your life, it is also important to be kind to yourself and not overtax yourself.

Before You Try Out Your Plan

As you anticipate your encounter with emotional claustrophobia, try to talk to yourself like this:

Soon I will face a situation which, in the past, filled me with fear of engulfment. Sometimes my emotional claustrophobia turned into rage and anger, sometimes into depression. Sometimes I stayed in the situation until I thought I would explode—or die. The situation was so distasteful, if not unbearable, that I promised myself I'd never put myself through the experience again. But I couldn't do that. Either because life—or a part of me—demands it of me, I have to face the situation again.

I am also aware that others don't experience emotional claustrophobia in this type of situation. This makes me feel abnormal, deviant, and different in a negative kind of way. But I need to remember there are reasons I react this way. I wasn't born with emotional claustrophobia, something started it and it wasn't my deficiencies.

The bad news is that my emotional claustrophobia has tarnished my joy of living. It also puts the brakes on some of my career and relationship goals. Yet managing my emotional claustrophobia by working on my levels of physical stress and my self-defeating thinking patterns takes a lot of effort. A part of me resents having to do all this work, but there's no choice, unless I want this fear to continue to limit my life.

The good news is that the coping methods work: I can lower my stress levels, begin to think in new ways about myself and communicate in a way that's strong and powerful, yet not abusive or mean. Although I can't control how others react, I can control my behavior the best I can.

I know that acting according to this plan (instead of reacting the old way) means taking certain risks. For example, if I use my plan in a situation that used to engulf me, I wonder how the situation will turn out using my new way of being. If I'm using the plan in a relationship, I wonder if I might damage, or even lose, the relationship. But if I continued to feel engulfed, I might start becoming angry or abusive or withdraw from the situation or from the other person emotionally. Then I might damage or lose the relationship anyway. If I don't take the risk of trying out these new ways, either I or the other person will most likely keep the relationship at a superficial level or cut it off entirely. If I feel smothered by a particular situation, I might lose my ability to be effective in it and abandon it, or I might be told by others that I am no longer needed.

I'm also afraid of the anxiety and fear I know I'm going to have when I start thinking and behaving according to my plan. What will happen? How will the other person react? How will I react? What will I feel if I don't feel the fear of engulfment? Will I feel some other scary feeling?

I'd like to avoid emotional pain and anxiety, but acting the old way won't save me from these feelings. In fact, it is the old ways that contributed to my pain and fears in the first place. At least the anxieties and fear that go along with changing my old ways of reacting will lead somewhere: to less fear of suffocation, or maybe no fear at all. The anxiety and fear attached to doing things the old way lead nowhere—except to the same old predictable pattern of having emotional claustrophobia control important parts of my life.

Immediately Before and During the Event

As you confront the event, try to speak to yourself as follows:

I need to take one step at a time. I can't think about the entire event or what might happen. I have to break it down into small segments, like five or ten minutes at a time. I also can't worry about whether or not I'm going to be "successful" in not feeling afraid. The very fact that I've taken the time to think through this type of incident, that I care enough about myself—and the other person, project, or effort—to try to deal with this fear is a success in itself.

I've visualized what usually happens and what I want to happen. My new beliefs, my breathing and relaxation exercises, and my vision of my safe place are there if I need them. I can call on them at any time. Yet I know that in the midst of this situation which has created so much fear in me in the past, I may not use these tools as often or as effectively as I planned.

However, if I change just one thing about how I usually act or think, that's a success. If I remember to take just a few deep breaths or to think about my new beliefs even once, then I'm a success. I've taken the first steps toward breaking a long history of reacting in a negative fashion. Even if I end up feeling engulfed, if I managed to change just one thing about how I usually act or think, I'm a success.

Changing one aspect of my thinking or acting may not seem like a major accomplishment, but it is. One small change will likely lead to more changes in the future. The next time I try out my plan, I may be able to change more of my behavior and attitudes so that I can take even better emotional care of myself in these kinds of situations. I need to give myself credit for facing the fear, rather than running from it or pretending that it doesn't matter.

I'll also be a success if I stay aware of my fears, anxieties, angers, and other feelings. I've done a lot of work on this situation and the difference between this situation and the events which caused me to have fear of engulfment in this type of situation is that _____ .

As I try to manage this fear of engulfment situation, I need to expect that my old self-defeating ways may persist, but I can remember new more liberating ways of thinking and believing and act as if these new beliefs are true. The beliefs which I especially need to focus on are _____ , _____ , *and* _____ .

I need to remember that I am not trying to hurt anyone, not myself or the person whom I'm with, not my performance or the effort with which I'm involved. I'm setting boundaries and handling this situation in a new way in order to overcome my emotional claustrophobia, but also to be able to participate more fully in certain activities and to have a more honest and potentially more meaningful relationship with another person. If I need to say something, I can do so in a nondefensive, kind way that doesn't abuse the other person or myself. I need to speak in terms of my needs and wishes, that is, in "I" messages.

If I feel uncomfortable or anxious relating in this new way, this does not mean I am a failure. I need to expect to be emotionally uncomfortable. After all, I'm in a trigger situation. Instead of getting mad at myself for starting to feel engulfed, I need to view these feelings as signals that I need to use one of my coping exercises. For example, it may be time to do some deep breathing exercises, call a friend, take time out, or whatever makes sense. I also need to remember the plan I made for handling this situation and stick with it.

Whenever I become overwhelmed with emotional claustrophobia and the anxiety and anger that go with it, I need to tell myself, "Everything's going to be okay. Eventually I can go somewhere where I feel safe."

Coping Methods During the Event

Keep in mind the following coping methods, which you can use as often as you need to:

- using relaxation, breathing techniques, and other self-calming methods

- visualizing your safe place

- replacing your self-defeating beliefs with more positive beliefs

- using emergency time-outs

- using one of your exit plans

- calling a friend

- acting as if you are someone else—someone you love and cherish

- sticking to the basics of your plan

- expecting the unexpected

In *Better Boundaries: Owning and Treasuring Your Life,* Jan Black and Greg Enns (1997) describe what they call the "person substitution" technique. It is highly recommended for people who are learning to be assertive and self-protective in situations that used to engulf them. The basic idea of this technique is that you pretend you are someone whom you cherish and want to protect, and act then in the same way you would want that person to act or as you envision that person acting.

For example, Lily was trying out her plan for managing her emotional claustrophobia during a family reunion where a certain aunt was pressuring her to stay longer than she wanted.

> *I wanted to get up and do something else, but I felt that I had to stay because of my aunt's sharp looks and biting remarks. I tried to ward her off by making small talk, but my fear of engulfment was rising and was beginning to take over my insides. I needed to take a break from the situation, but I didn't feel I could excuse myself.*
>
> *Then I thought of my daughter. Would I want her to feel trapped like this? No. I'd want her to politely excuse herself and go do what she wanted or needed to do. Thinking about it, I realize that's what my aunt does. She doesn't feel trapped by me, or anyone else. When she wants to do something, she just does it, even abruptly so, without a song and dance. If my daughter and aunt can feel free, so can I—without a million excuses.*

Acknowledging Reality

Setting up boundaries in a relationship where there were no boundaries or unclear, vague boundaries before will make an impact on the relationship. In some cases, no matter how well-planned and nonattacking your communication is, what you say will cause alienation and hurt. If the other person interprets your setting boundaries as a form of rejection, despite your clear statements to the contrary, that individual may lash back at you, feign indifference, and reject you. The more attached that individual is to you, the greater his or her sense of perceived loss, the more violent the reaction to your setting your limits and taking care of yourself is likely to be. Also, the more attached you are to that individual, the greater the sense of loss you will feel if he or she responds negatively to your declaration of your boundaries.

Such situations are painful for all concerned. However, if you have spoken about your needs and limits in terms of yourself, not the other person, and you've presented them in a nonhostile, calm manner, you have done all you can to minimize any pain that might result from your interaction. Furthermore, by communicating openly you have shown that you care. Setting boundaries is a self-affirming act, but it is also an act that says, "I am different from you. If we are to have a relationship, I have certain needs that must be respected." This act of separating from the other person can feel like a loss, at least initially, both for the other person and for you.

One possibility is that the pain caused by setting boundaries is, in effect, the growing pains of a relationship that will be closer and more intimate and satisfying precisely because you have set limits and spoken up. However, setting boundaries won't always yield an improved relationship. Not everyone will feel comfortable with the limits you set and some people will reject or distance themselves from you. In some cases, the alienation may be short-lived; in others, it may be long-term or permanent.

You may be told, or made to understand in other ways, that if you want to be part of the family, group, or relationship again, you will need to abandon your means of taking care of yourself and return to the old way of relating, the way that led to your fear of engulfment. In such situations, the unhappy choice is yours: coping with fear of engulfment or coping with the sense of loss that comes when relationships that matter are weakened or dying. One option is to give the relationship time. If someone makes it clear to you that they do not wish to be connected with you unless you give up some of your boundaries, then you can respect their need to distance themselves from you and leave them alone. However, you can also contact them after some time has passed and offer to renew the relationship, but not by compromising your needs.

Keep in mind that you are responsible for your life. There may come a time when you must think about yourself, as well as others, and be primarily concerned with your well-being. All relationships need to be based on mutual caring and mutual respect, which involves honoring each other's feelings, needs, and limitations. According to Paul Tournier (1977) there are two types of guilt: true guilt and false guilt. False guilt refers to feelings of guilt that result from not living up to the expectations of others; true guilt, from not having lived up to your true potential and from having failed to take care of, protect, and nurture yourself.

If you find yourself in emotional pain as you try to be your self and as you slowly say goodbye to your emotional claustrophobia, remember that part of recovery involves grieving your lost self. Try not to interpret the pain involved with growth as a sign that you are a psychological failure and that all of your efforts have been in vain. If you honestly face the feelings involved with the process of recovery and of losing part of your old identity, these feelings will eventually pass.

While your new behavior may have an effect on others, do not be surprised if the steps you are taking to help yourself go unnoticed or are dismissed. For example, Ali wondered how to tell his relatives that he wanted to stay in a hotel rather than at their home. In some families, it is considered overly demanding or intrusive for out-of-town visitors to expect to stay with their relatives. But in Ali's culture, it was considered an insult to one's relatives to stay at a hotel, rather than at their home. Ali didn't want to hurt his relatives, but he knew from experience that staying with them resulted in such strong feelings of emotional claustrophobia that he almost didn't want to visit them anymore:

> *I need some space from them if I'm to enjoy them. But they'll give me such grief if I stay at a hotel, my visit might be ruined. Maybe if I find the right way to tell them, I'll be spared the criticisms and interrogations.*
>
> *As I planned what to say, I agonized to find the right words. I wanted to state my needs without being defensive but also without blaming them or making any negative statements about them or statements that they might interpret negatively. The usual pop-psychology things to say with regular Americans wouldn't work with my relatives: they're from the old country. What might not be accusing or blaming to most people here would be to them.*
>
> *To spare their feelings and make it easier on me, I considered lying to them, for example, telling them that I had*

won two free nights at a hotel. But I didn't feel good about that. I thought about it and thought about it and finally decided to tell them something emotionally neutral and personally vague, like that staying at a hotel "would be best for me." If they asked a lot of questions or pressed the point, which I was sure they would, I'd just repeat, "I know you want me to stay and that makes me feel so wanted. I'm so lucky to have relatives who are so generous. But this time I need to stay at a hotel. It works best for me."

As I rehearsed what I was going to say and envisioned their predictable negative responses, I would become so anxious I nearly forgot what it was I had planned to say. So I wrote everything down on paper and periodically reviewed my lines. Despite all this practice, there were times I'd start feeling smothered by the prospect of confronting them.

The day I actually told them, despite all my preparation, my mind went blank. I was positive I wouldn't be able to speak at all and that I would cancel my hotel reservations and stay at their house. When I opened my mouth, I felt numb and spaced out, as if I was in a play about my life rather than in my life. Then, wonder of wonders, I actually said what I had planned to say and it sounded good, too: kind and loving, yet firm. I had been so worried that if I said anything, I'd sound like a frightened child or an angry self-centered one.

Then, even more amazing, my relatives didn't respond at all. They stared at me for a minute, then changed the subject. Maybe they couldn't handle it, maybe they didn't know what to say, or maybe they didn't want to alienate me. Whatever the reason, I stayed at the hotel without any negative overt reaction. I was shocked that they seemed so neutral about it, but also very pleased. I was especially pleased with myself for being able to like the person I wanted to be: someone who could respect his limitations and take care of himself without being defensive or apologetic and without being nasty or alienating others either.

Ali also found that when he set limits on his commitment to his part-time job, that his employer made no comment. "To think that I could have suffered doing more than I could handle just because I was afraid to speak up. I've learned that sometimes when I set my boundaries, people become angry and revolt. But other times, they accept my limits without interrogating or punishing me."

Taking Stock

After you have tried out one of your plans, take stock. In your journal on a fresh piece of paper entitled "Taking Stock," answer the following questions:

Taking Stock

After you have tried out one of your plans, take stock. In your journal on a fresh piece of paper entitled "Taking Stock," answer the following questions:

• What did you do differently this time than other times? Did you remember to use your deep breathing or other self-calming methods? Which ones did you use? Which ones helped? Which ones didn't help?

• What were you thinking during the event? Were you able to remember some of your desired beliefs? (Give yourself credit for being able to remember your desired beliefs, even if the self-defeating beliefs flooded your mind and you were unable to act on your desired beliefs.)

• Did you use your communication skills: "I" messages, boundary setting, affirming the positives of your connection with the other person, avoiding verbal abuse? Even if you only managed *one* "I" message or managed to make one positive statement to the other person, give yourself credit.

• Were you able to take a time-out or break when you needed to? If not, what prevented you?

• What did you learn from this experience? How would you handle the same situation next time?

• How did it feel to exert control, even a little control, over the situation?

• How afraid of being engulfed did you feel during the experience? Afterward? Do not be surprised if you are afraid sometimes but not afraid other times.

• What other feelings did you have during the experience? Afterward? Do not be surprised if you experienced a mix of feelings: from relief and elation at having overcome some of your fear of engulfment to depression, sadness, or anger.

• Were you surprised to feel afraid of the change or to find yourself missing your old claustrophobic self? Are you able to accept that there is anxiety and a sense of loss about any change, even positive change? What was the source of your anxiety: what did you fear would happen because you reacted differently? What was the source of your sense of loss? What have you actually lost and what have you actually gained as the result of applying your new coping techniques and adhering to your desired beliefs?

- What effect did your new behaviors have on the other person? In your judgment, will this be a short-term or long-term effect? Is there anything more you'd like to do to help improve your relationships with that individual, without retracting your boundaries?

- What effect did your new behaviors have on the project you are working on or the other efforts with which you are involved? Based on what you can observe and any feedback you've received from others, will this be a short-term or long-term effect? Are there other ways to improve your participation in this effort without ignoring your limitations and personal needs?

Reviewing Your Progress

Over the course of this book, you have had the courage to look at your emotional claustrophobia. You have identified some of the causes of your fear and, as the result of this knowledge, you are no longer in the dark about certain important aspects of your life. You have learned some means of calming yourself physically so that when you start to become afraid, you are no longer helpless in the face of mounting physical tension. You have also worked on identifying self-defeating beliefs and replacing them with beliefs that affirm your worth, the worthiness of life, and your ability to act on your own behalf and affirm yourself. The communication skills you have practiced have helped you interact in an emotionally honest but nonabusive manner with others.

You have also surmounted perhaps the biggest obstacle of all—embracing the uncertainty and emotional turmoil involved with choosing change over old patterns of thought and behavior, which although painful and limiting, are at least familiar, and in that sense, "comfortable." "I've come to see that no experience in life is wholly good or wholly bad; all experiences have elements of both. ... Do you have a problem? Take heart—maybe what you really have is an opportunity" (Greene 1999).

If you are suffering, having someone suggest that you can make lemonade out of the lemons life has handed you may make you feel like he or she is discounting your pain.

Sometimes you can try with all your might to turn the lemons into lemonade, and you find it is impossible. There are many circumstances where whatever "good" is evident is minuscule, or feels minuscule, to the amount of "bad" that still exists. However, at the very least, the process of trying to wrest some good out of the difficulties in your life, difficulties such as emotional cluaustophobia, can get you motivated to reevaluate your life and personal goals.

You need to give yourself credit for all of these accomplishments. The more you practice the coping skills you have learned and the more you start thinking about emotional claustrophobia in ways that promote, rather than hinder, your self-worth and personal development, the more natural it will feel to use these coping skills. If you continue facing your fears and following the types of plans you have made in this book, over time you won't have to work so hard to get through situations that cause you to feel smothered or to deal with people whom you find smothering. If you keep practicing your coping techniques and thinking in terms of your new beliefs, you will be creating a new history for yourself. Eventually the new history will be more familiar and powerful than the old history, and emotional claustrophobia will inhibit your life less and less.

Appendix

The organizations and materials listed here are by no means all the resources available. This list is only a beginning. In some categories there are hundreds of books available. I encourage you to look beyond this list on your own. Spend some time on the Internet or at your local library, and ask the librarian for assistance if you need it. Also talk to helping professionals to see what resources they can recommend.

Anger Management

McKay, Matthew, Judith McKay, and Peter Rogers. 1989. *When Anger Hurts: Quieting the Storm Within*. Oakland, Calif.: New Harbinger Publications.

Matsakis, Aphrodite. 1996. I *Can't Get Over It: A Handbook for Trauma Survivors*. Oakland, Calif.: New Harbinger Publications.

Battering—Family Violence

Agencies and Organizations

You can be directed to sources of help by courts, social service agencies, churches, battered women's shelters, or state chapters of the National Coalition Against Domestic Violence. Call 303-839-1852, the national office of the coalition, for information about your state chapter, or check your local phone directory. You may also be able to get names and phone numbers of sources of assistance from your local police, local library, community crisis center, or mental health hotline. If you have difficulties locating help in your community, contact the National Domestic Violence Hotline, 1-800-700 SAFE (or 1-800-799-7233) or contact the coalition at P.O. Box 161810, Austin, Texas 78716.

It may be helpful for you to contact the National Organization for Victim Assistance, 1757 Park Road N.W., Washington, D.C., 20010; 202-232-6682. The crisis line is 1-800-TRY-NOVA. This organization can provide crisis intervention, short-term counseling, medical and legal advice, and referrals to some 8,000 victim-assistance programs across the country, including battered women's programs and rape crisis centers.

Books and Other Materials

Black, Jan, and Gregg Enns. 1997. *It's Not Okay Anymore, Your Personal Guide to Ending Abuse: Taking Charge and Loving Yourself.* Oakland, Calif.: New Harbinger Publications.

Martin, Del. 1981. *Battered Wives.* San Francisco, Calif.: Volcano Press.

Ni Carthy, Ginny. 1986. *Getting Free: A Handbook for Women in Abusive Relationships.* Seattle: Seal Press.

Walker, Lenore. 1979. *The Battered Woman.* New York: Harper and Row.

White, Evelyn. 1985. *Chain Chain Change: For Black Women Dealing with Physical and Emotional Abuse.* Seattle: Seal Press.

Zambrano, Myrna, M. 1985. *Major Sola Que Mal Acompanada: Para La Mujer Golopeada/For the Latina in an Abusive Relationship.* Seattle: Seal Press.

Child Abuse

Agencies and Organizations

The National Child Abuse Hotline (800-442-4453), run by Childhelp USA, provides on-the-spot telephone counseling to any child being abused (physically or sexually) and offers immediate assistance, information, and referrals to anyone concerned about abused children (e.g., neighbors, friends, school, and other officials, and survivors of past abuse). Childhelp USA's address is 15757 North 78th Street, Scottsdale, Arizona 85360.

Books and Other Materials

Numerous books, pamphlets, and workbooks on recovering from physical and/or sexual abuse are available from Hazelden Educational Materials, Box 176, Pleasant Valley Road, Center City, MN 55012. Call 800-328-9000 for a free catalog.

Bass, Ellen, and Laura Davis. 1988. *The Courage to Heal*, New York: Harper and Row.

Adams, Caren, and Jennifer Fay. 1989. *Free of the Shadows: Recovering from Sexual Violence.* Oakland, Calif.: New Harbinger Publications.

Courtois, Christine. 1997. *Adult Survivors of Child Sexual Abuse.* Milwaukee, Wisc.: Families International.

Engel, Beverly. 1989. *The Right to Innocence: Healing the Trauma of Sexual Abuse.* New York: Ivy.

"Everything You Always Wanted to Know about Child Abuse and Neglect." Available from the National Center on Child Abuse and Neglect, Department of Health and Human Services, P.O. Box 1182, Washington, D.C. Also available from the same address is a listing of free and low-cost pamphlets on child abuse and neglect.

Farmer, Steven. 1989. *Adult Children of Abusive Parents.* Los Angeles, Calif.: Lowell House.

Matsakis, Aphrodite. 1994. *When the Bough Breaks: A Helping Guide for Parents of Sexually Abused Children.* Oakland, Calif.: New Harbinger Publications.

Kunzman, Kristin. 1990. *The Healing Way—Adult Recovery from Childhood Sexual Abuse.* Center City, Minn.: Hazelden Educational Materials.

Lew, Michael. 1989. *Victims No Longer: Men Recovering from Incest and Other Sexual Abuse.* New York: Nevramont Publishing Co.

Matsakis, Aphrodite. 1996. *I Can't Get Over It: A Handbook for Trauma Survivors.* Oakland, Calif.: New Harbinger Publications.

Matsakis, Aphrodite. 1998. *Trust After Trauma: A Relationship Guide for Trauma Survivors and Those Who Love Them.* Oakland, Calif.: New Harbinger Publications.

Nice, Suzanne, and Russell Forset. 1990. *Childhood Sexual Abuse: A Survivor's Guide for Men.* Center City, Minn.: Hazelden Educational Materials.

Ratne, Ellen. 1990. *The Other Side of the Family: A Book of Recovery from Abuse, Incest, and Neglect.* Deerfield Beach, Fl.: Health Communications.

Guidelines for Interacting/Confronting Abusive Family Members

For Lay Persons

Davis, Laura. 1990. *The Courage to Heal Workbook.* New York: Harper and Row.

For Professionals

Courtois, Christine. 1988. *Healing the Incest Wound.* New York: W. W. Norton

Depression

Books and Other Materials

Burns, David D. 1980. *Feeling Good: The New Mood Therapy.* New York: Signet Books.

Presnall, Louis. 1985. *First Aid for Depression.* Center City, Minn.: Hazelden Educational Materials.

Rosellini, Gail, and Mark Warden. 1988. *Here Comes the Sun.* Center City, Minn.: Hazelden Educational Materials.

Rape and Sexual Assault

Agencies and Organizations

Contact your local rape crisis center, police station, or social services department for assistance, information, and support. If your area does not have a rape crisis center, see if there is a battered women's shelter available.

Books and Other Materials

Fay, Jennifer, and Caren Adams. *Free of the Shadows: Recovering from Sexual Violence.* 1989. Oakland, Calif.: New Harbinger Publications.

Ledray, Linda. 1986. *Recovering from Rape.* New York: Owl Books, Henry Holt and Company.

Lew, Mike. 1988. *Victims No Longer: Men Recovering from Incest and Other Sexual Abuse.* New York: Nevramont Publishing Co.

McEvoy, Alan, and Jeff Brookings. 1984. *If She Is Raped: A Book for Husbands, Fathers, and Male Friends.* Holmes Beach, Fl.: Learning Publications, Inc.

Warshaw, Robin. 1988. *I Never Called It Rape.* New York: Harper and Row.

Relaxation: Anxiety and Panic Disorders Management

Organizations

The Anxiety Disorders Association of America (ADAA), 1900 Parklawn Drive, Suite 100, Rockville, MD 20852-2624. 301-231 9350. Web site: www.adaa.org

Books and Other Materials

Bourne, Edmund. 2000. *Anxiety and Phobia Workbook,* Third Edition. Oakland, Calif.: New Harbinger Publications.

Miller, Emmett. *Letting Go of Stress.* Audiocassette available from Source, 945 Evelyn Street, Menlo Park, Calif. 94025; 800-528-2737, or 415-328-7171 in California.

McKay, Matthew, Elizabeth R. Eshelman, and Martha Davis. 2000. *The Relaxation and Stress Reduction Workbook,* Fifth Edition. Oakland, Calif.: New Harbinger Publications.

Nudzynski, Thomas. *Relaxation Training Program.* (three cassette set). Available from Guilford Publications, 72 Spring Street, New York, N.Y. 10012; 800-365-7006, or 212-431-9800 in New York.

Zuercher-White, Elke. 1998. *An End to Panic: Breakthrough Techniques for Overcoming Panic Disorder,* Second Edition, Oakland, Calif.: New Harbinger Publications.

Self-Esteem and Assertiveness

Black, Jan, and Greg Enns. 1997. *Better Boundaries: Owning and Treasuring Your Life.* Oakland, Calif.: New Harbinger Publications.

Butler, P. E. 1992. *Self-Assertion for Women.* San Francisco, Calif.: Harper and Row.

McKay, Matthew, and Patrick Fanning. 1991. *Prisoners of Belief: Exposing and Changing Beliefs That Control Your Life.* Oakland, Calif.: New Harbinger Publications.

McKay, Matthew and Patrick Fanning. 1993. *Self Esteem,* Second Edition. Oakland: Calif.: New Harbinger Publications.

McKay, Matthew, Patrick Fanning, Carole Honeychurch, and Catharine Sutker. 1999. *The Self-Esteem Companion.* Oakland, Calif.: New Harbinger Publications.

Smith, Manuel J. 1975. *When I Say No I Feel Guilty.* New York: Bantam Books.

Trauma Processing

Matsakis, Aphrodite. 1991. *Post-Traumatic Stress Disorder: A Complete Treatment Guide.* Oakland, Calif.: New Harbinger Publications.

Matsakis, Aphrodite. 1996. *I Can't Get Over It: A Handbook for Trauma Survivors.* Oakland, Calif.: New Harbinger Publications.

Matsakis, Aphrodite. 1998. *Trust After Trauma: A Relationship Guide for Trauma Survivors and Those Who Love Them.* Oakland, Calif.: New Harbinger Publications.

Matsakis, Aphrodite. 1999. *Survivor Guilt: A Self-Help Guide.* Oakland, Calif.: New Harbinger Publications.

References

Bass, Ellen, and Laura Davis. 1988. *The Courage To Heal.* New York: Harber and Row.

Black, Jan, and Greg Enns. 1997. *Better Boundaries: Owning and Treasuring Your Life.* Oakland, Calif.: New Harbinger Publications.

Bourne, Edmund J. 2000. *The Anxiety and Phobia Workbook,* Third Edition Oakland, Calif.: New Harbinger Publications.

Campbell, Joseph. 1988. *The Power of Myth.* New York: Doubleday.

Courtois, Christine.1988. *Healing the Incest Wound: Adult Survivors in Therapy.* New York: W.W. Norton.

Davis, Laura. 1990. *The Courage to Heal Workbook.* New York: Harper and Row.

Davis, Martha, Elizabeth Eshelman, and Matthew McKay. 2000. *The Relaxation and Stress Reduction Workbook,* Fifth Edition. Oakland, Calif.: New Harbinger Publications.

Goldstein, Amy, and Roberto Suro. 2000. "A Journey in Stages: Assimilation's Pull is Still Strong, but Its Pace Varies." *Washington Post,* January 16.

Greene, Bernie. 1999. "Pain, Paradox, and Serendipity." Wheaton, Md.: Unpublished manuscript.

Harvey, Claire. 1995. "Stories of Resiliency in Trauma Survivors." Audiotape 951STSS: International Society for Traumatic Stress Studies, 11th Annual Meeting. Boston, Mass.

Herman, Judith. 1992. *Trauma and Recovery*. New York: Basic Books.

James, Beverly. 1994. "Trauma in Infants, Children, and Adolescents: Context and Connectedness." Audiotape 96ISTSS-1: International Society for Traumatic Stress, 10th Annual Meeting. San Francisco, Calif..

Kerr, Michael, and Murray Bowen. 1988. *Family Evaluation*. New York: W. W. Norton.

Kubler-Ross, Elisabeth. 1969. *On Death and Dying*. New York: Macmillan Publishing Company.

La Franiere, Sharon. 2000. "In Russia: Therapy for Cloying Closeness." *Washington Post,* January 3.

Lerner, Harriet. 1985. *The Dance of Anger, A Woman's Guide to Changing the Patterns of Intimate Relationships*. New York: Harper and Row.

Matsakis, Aphrodite. 1996. *Vietnam Wives: Facing the Challenges of Life with Veterans Suffering Post-Traumatic Stress*, Second Edition. Lutherville, Md.: The Sidran Foundation.

Matsakis, Aphrodite. 1996. *I Can't Get Over It: A Handbook for Trauma Survivors, Second Edition.* Oakland, Calif.: New Harbinger Publications.

McKay, Matthew, and Patrick Fanning. 1991. *Prisoners of Belief: Exposing and Changing Beliefs That Control Your Life*. Oakland, Calif.: New Harbinger Publications.

McKay, Matthew, Peter Rogers, and Judith McKay. 1989. *When Anger Hurts: Quieting the Storm Within*. Oakland, Calif.: New Harbinger Publications.

Pearlman, Laura. 1994. "Trauma and the Fulfillment of Human Potential." Audiotape, International Society for Traumatic Stress, 10th Annual Meeting, San Francisco, CA.

Rosenheck, Robert, and P. Nathan. 1985. "Secondary Traumatization in the Children of Vietnam Veterans with Posttraumatic Stress Disorder." *Hospital and Community Psychiatry* 36:538–539.

Rosenheck, Robert. 1986. "Impact of PTSD of World War II on the Next Generation." *Journal of Nervous and Mental Disease.* 174:319–327.

Silverman, Joel L. 1986. "Post Traumatic Stress Disorder." *Advanced Psychosomatic Medicine* 16:115–140.

Smith, Barry D. 1998. *Psychology: Science and Understanding.* New York: McGraw-Hill.

Steinbeck, John. 1976. *The Pearl.* New York: Penguin Books.

Tournier, Paul. 1977. *The Best of Tournier.* New York: Harper and Row.

Zuercher-White, Elke. 1998. *An End to Panic: Breakthrough Techniques for Overcoming Panic Disorder,* Second Edition. Oakland, Calif.: New Harbinger Publications.

van der Kolk, Bessel A., Alexander McFarlane, and Lars Weisaeth. 1996. "The Black Hole of Trauma." In *Traumatic Stress: Effects of Overwhelming Experience on Mind, Body, and Society.* New York: The Guilford Press.

 As a specialist in post-traumatic stress disorder, Aphrodite Matsakis, Ph.D., has counseled thousands of clients ranging from combat veterans to victims of crime and abuse and other traumatic events. She conducts a private psychotherapy practice specializing in post-traumatic stress disorder, child abuse, depression, anxiety disorders, chronic pain, and couple and family therapy.

Related Titles: Matsakis has helped tens of thousands of individuals through her popular books, which include *Trust After Trauma, Survivor Guilt, I Can't Get Over It, When the Bough Breaks,* and *Post-Traumatic Stress Disorder.*

Also by Aphrodite Matsakis

SURVIVOR GUILT

Helps survivors come to terms with feelings of guilt and cope with how they affect their personal functioning and relationships.   *Item SG $14.95*

TRUST AFTER TRAUMA

Step-by-step exercises help readers manage emotions, handle unresolved issues, and end self-perpetuating cycles of withdrawal and isolation.   *Item TAT Paperback $15.95*

I CAN'T GET OVER IT

The second edition of this groundbreaking work guides readers through the healing process of recovering from PTSD one step at a time.   *Item OVER Paperback $16.95*

WHEN THE BOUGH BREAKS

Provides the information parents need to identify sexual abuse, deal with the reactions of others, and help children cope and heal.   *Item BOU $14.95*

MANAGING CLIENT ANGER

This professional guide helps therapists understand their reactions to client anger and make constructive interventions.   *Item MCA $49.95*

POST-TRAUMATIC STRESS DISORDER

This professional guide balances symptom management and emotional control with work aimed at reexperiencing feelings and healing the effects of trauma.   *Item CANT Hardcover $49.95*

Call **toll-free 1-800-748-6273** to order. Have your Visa or Mastercard number ready. Or send a check for the titles you want to New Harbinger Publications, 5674 Shattuck Avenue, Oakland, CA 94609. Include $3.80 for the first book and 75¢ for each additional book to cover shipping and handling. (California residents please include appropriate sales tax.) Allow four to six weeks for delivery.

Prices subject to change without notice.

Some Other New Harbinger Self-Help Titles

Multiple Chemical Sensitivity: A Survival Guide, $16.95
Dancing Naked, $14.95
Why Are We Still Fighting, $15.95
From Sabotage to Success, $14.95
Parkinson's Disease and the Art of Moving, $15.95
A Survivor's Guide to Breast Cancer, $13.95
Men, Women, and Prostate Cancer, $15.95
Make Every Session Count: Getting the Most Out of Your Brief Therapy, $10.95
Virtual Addiction, $12.95
After the Breakup, $13.95
Why Can't I Be the Parent I Want to Be?, $12.95
The Secret Message of Shame, $13.95
The OCD Workbook, $18.95
Tapping Your Inner Strength, $13.95
Binge No More, $14.95
When to Forgive, $12.95
Practical Dreaming, $12.95
Healthy Baby, Toxic World, $15.95
Making Hope Happen, $14.95
I'll Take Care of You, $12.95
Survivor Guilt, $14.95
Children Changed by Trauma, $13.95
Understanding Your Child's Sexual Behavior, $12.95
The Self-Esteem Companion, $10.95
The Gay and Lesbian Self-Esteem Book, $13.95
Making the Big Move, $13.95
How to Survive and Thrive in an Empty Nest, $13.95
Living Well with a Hidden Disability, $15.95
Overcoming Repetitive Motion Injuries the Rossiter Way, $15.95
What to Tell the Kids About Your Divorce, $13.95
The Divorce Book, Second Edition, $15.95
Claiming Your Creative Self: True Stories from the Everyday Lives of Women, $15.95
Six Keys to Creating the Life You Desire, $19.95
Taking Control of TMJ, $13.95
What You Need to Know About Alzheimer's, $15.95
Winning Against Relapse: A Workbook of Action Plans for Recurring Health and Emotional Problems, $14.95
Facing 30: Women Talk About Constructing a Real Life and Other Scary Rites of Passage, $12.95
The Worry Control Workbook, $15.95
Wanting What You Have: A Self-Discovery Workbook, $18.95
When Perfect Isn't Good Enough: Strategies for Coping with Perfectionism, $13.95
Earning Your Own Respect: A Handbook of Personal Responsibility, $12.95
High on Stress: A Woman's Guide to Optimizing the Stress in Her Life, $13.95
Infidelity: A Survival Guide, $13.95
Stop Walking on Eggshells, $14.95
Consumer's Guide to Psychiatric Drugs, $16.95
The Fibromyalgia Advocate: Getting the Support You Need to Cope with Fibromyalgia and Myofascial Pain, $18.95
Healing Fear: New Approaches to Overcoming Anxiety, $16.95
Working Anger: Preventing and Resolving Conflict on the Job, $12.95
Sex Smart: How Your Childhood Shaped Your Sexual Life and What to Do About It, $14.95
You Can Free Yourself From Alcohol & Drugs, $13.95
Amongst Ourselves: A Self-Help Guide to Living with Dissociative Identity Disorder, $14.95
Healthy Living with Diabetes, $13.95
Dr. Carl Robinson's Basic Baby Care, $10.95
Better Boundries: Owning and Treasuring Your Life, $13.95
Goodbye Good Girl, $12.95
Fibromyalgia & Chronic Myofascial Pain Syndrome, $19.95
The Depression Workbook: Living With Depression and Manic Depression, $17.95
Self-Esteem, Second Edition, $13.95
Angry All the Time: An Emergency Guide to Anger Control, $12.95
When Anger Hurts, $13.95
Perimenopause, $16.95
The Relaxation & Stress Reduction Workbook, Fourth Edition, $17.95
The Anxiety & Phobia Workbook, Second Edition, $18.95
I Can't Get Over It, A Handbook for Trauma Survivors, Second Edition, $16.95
Messages: The Communication Skills Workbook, Second Edition, $15.95
Thoughts & Feelings, Second Edition, $18.95
Depression: How It Happens, How It's Healed, $14.95
The Deadly Diet, Second Edition, $14.95
The Power of Two, $15.95

Call **toll free, 1-800-748-6273,** or log on to our online bookstore at **www.newharbinger.com** to order. Have your Visa or Mastercard number ready. Or send a check for the titles you want to New Harbinger Publications, Inc., 5674 Shattuck Ave., Oakland, CA 94609. Include $3.80 for the first book and 75¢ for each additional book, to cover shipping and handling. (California residents please include appropriate sales tax.) Allow two to five weeks for delivery.

Prices subject to change without notice.